THE OFFICIAL

HIBERNIAN Football Club

ANNUAL 2023

Designed by: Jon Dalrymple

A Grange Publication

Printed in the EU.

ISBN 978-1-915295-49-1

CONTENTS

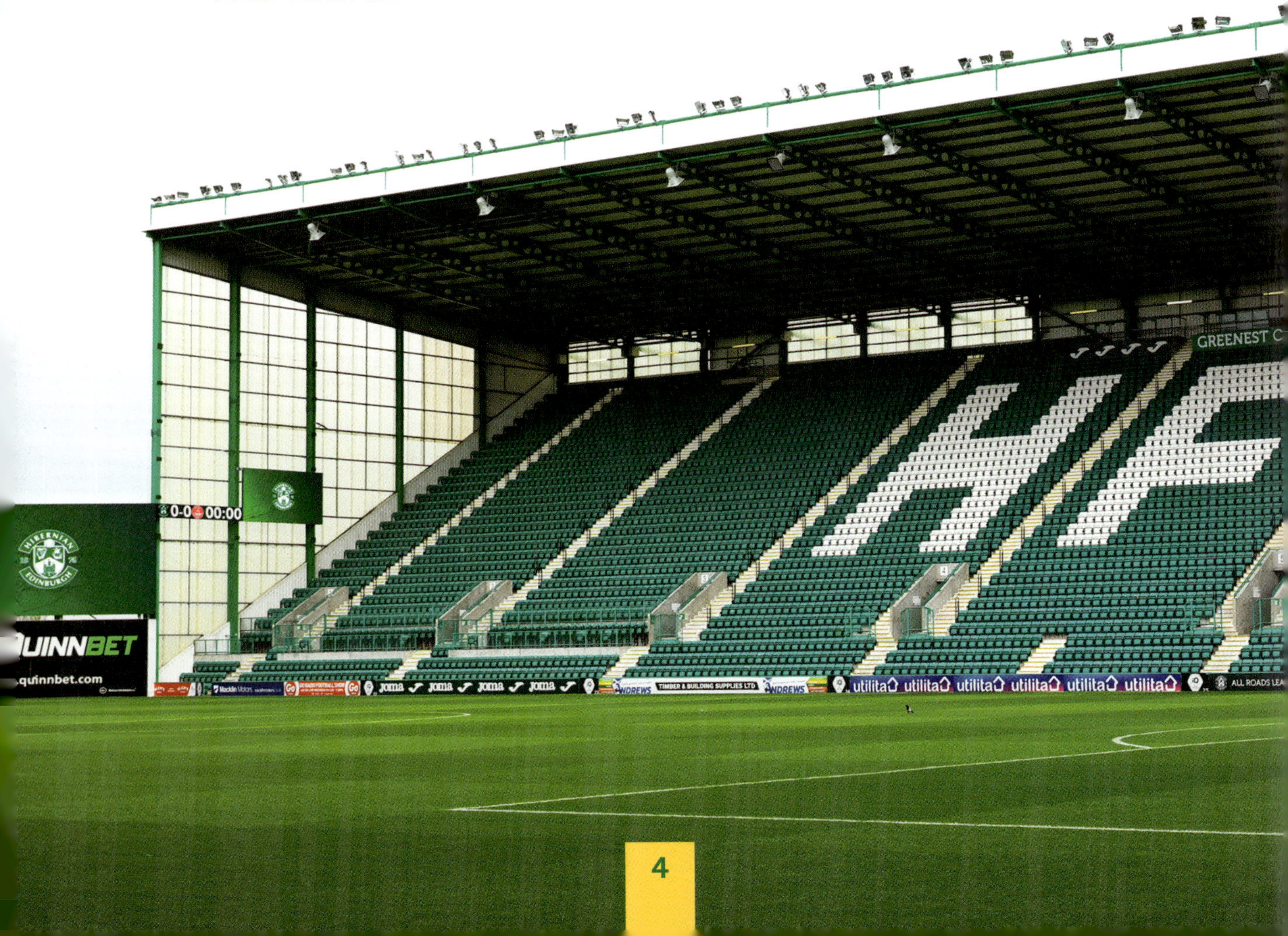

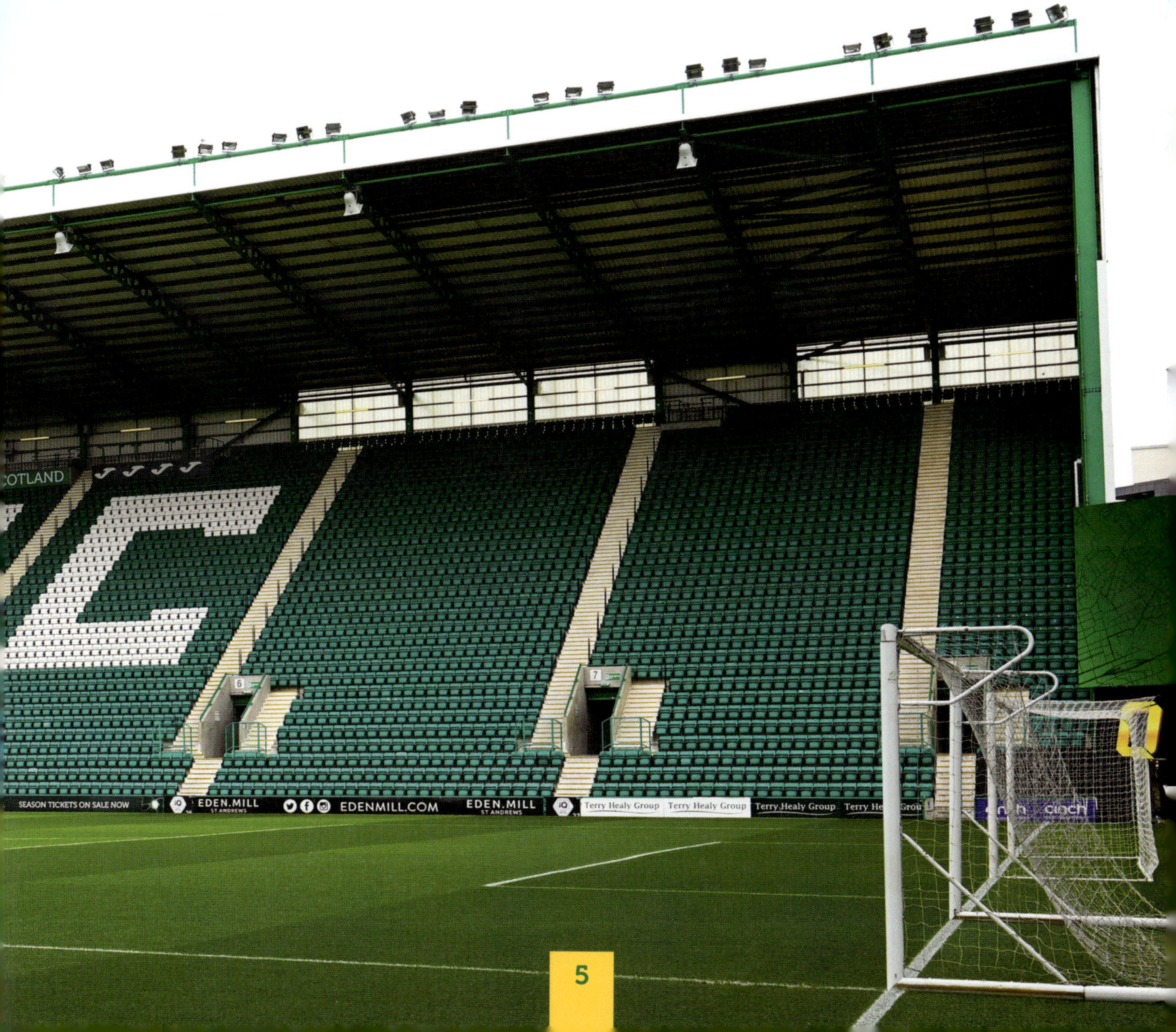
SEASON TICKETS ON SALE NOW
EDEN.MILL
EDENMILL.COM
EDEN.MILL
Terry Healy Group
Terry Healy Group
Terry Healy Group

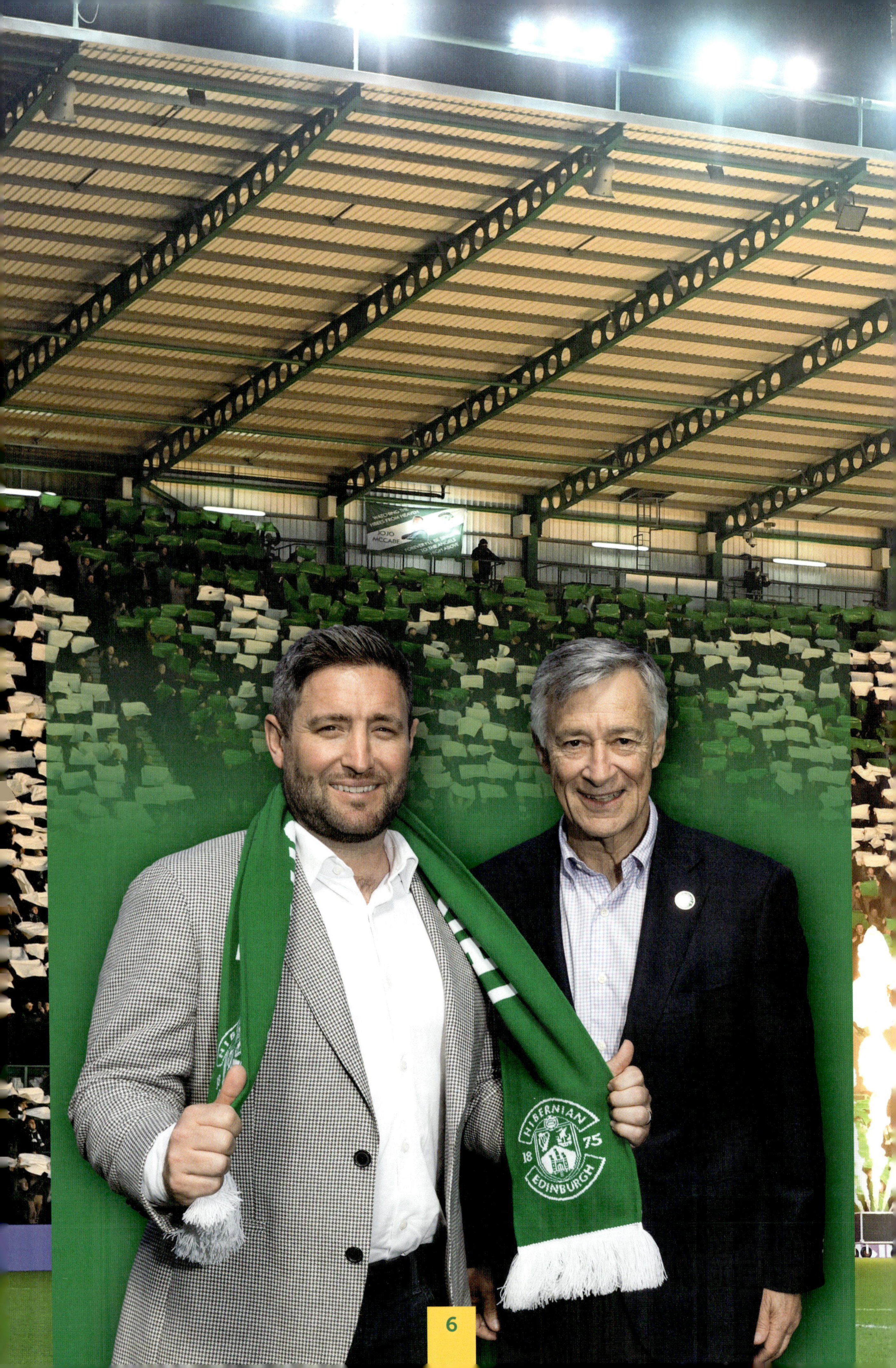
JOJO MCCABE
HIBERNIAN
18
75
EDINBURGH

WELCOME

Welcome to the latest edition of the official Hibernian FC annual!

As ever, we'll look back on an eventful season at Easter Road which, thankfully, saw the return of supporters after the easing of Covid-19 restrictions.

We'll test your knowledge of the most recent campaign and the current squad with our quizzes and you can get to know two little-known members of the backroom staff a little better.

We'll celebrate the contribution of two modern-day legends in Lewis Stevenson and Paul Hanlon, while profiling Kevin Dabrowski and Kevin Nisbet.

Hibernian Women continue to go from strength to strength. We checked in with Leah Eddie for the latest.

With so many uncertainties in the world over the last year or two, what has been consistent is the efforts of the wider Hibernian family within the community, so we'll shine a light on the work being done by the Hibernian Community Foundation and Dnipro Kids.

With Lee Johnson in place as manager and some ambitious plans for the club, on and off the pitch, it's an exciting time to be a Hibee.

The annual will bring you up to speed with everything you need to know about the club you love.

HIGHLIGHTS OF THE SEASON

JULY

The 2-1 pre-season friendly win over Arsenal was memorable for a good performance – but made all the more significant by the return of supporters to Easter Road Stadium after 16 long months. Some 2000 were able to enjoy the occasion.

Paul Hanlon was officially named club captain following David Gray's switch to the coaching staff, and it was another proud moment for the boyhood Hibee who has lived the dream.

Hibs made it to the third qualifying round of the UEFA Europa Conference League after a 5-1 aggregate victory over Andorran's FC Santa Coloma.

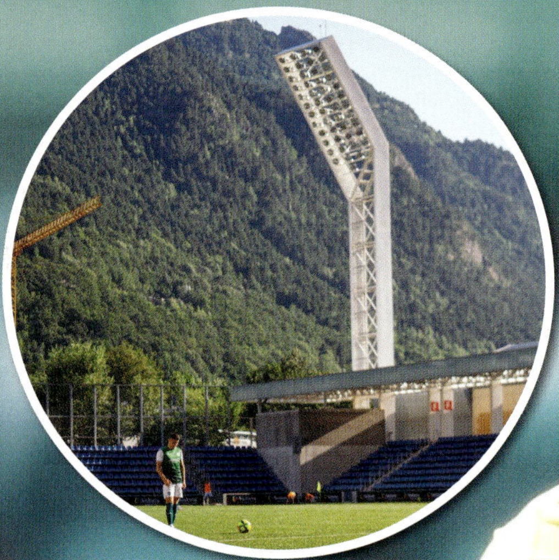

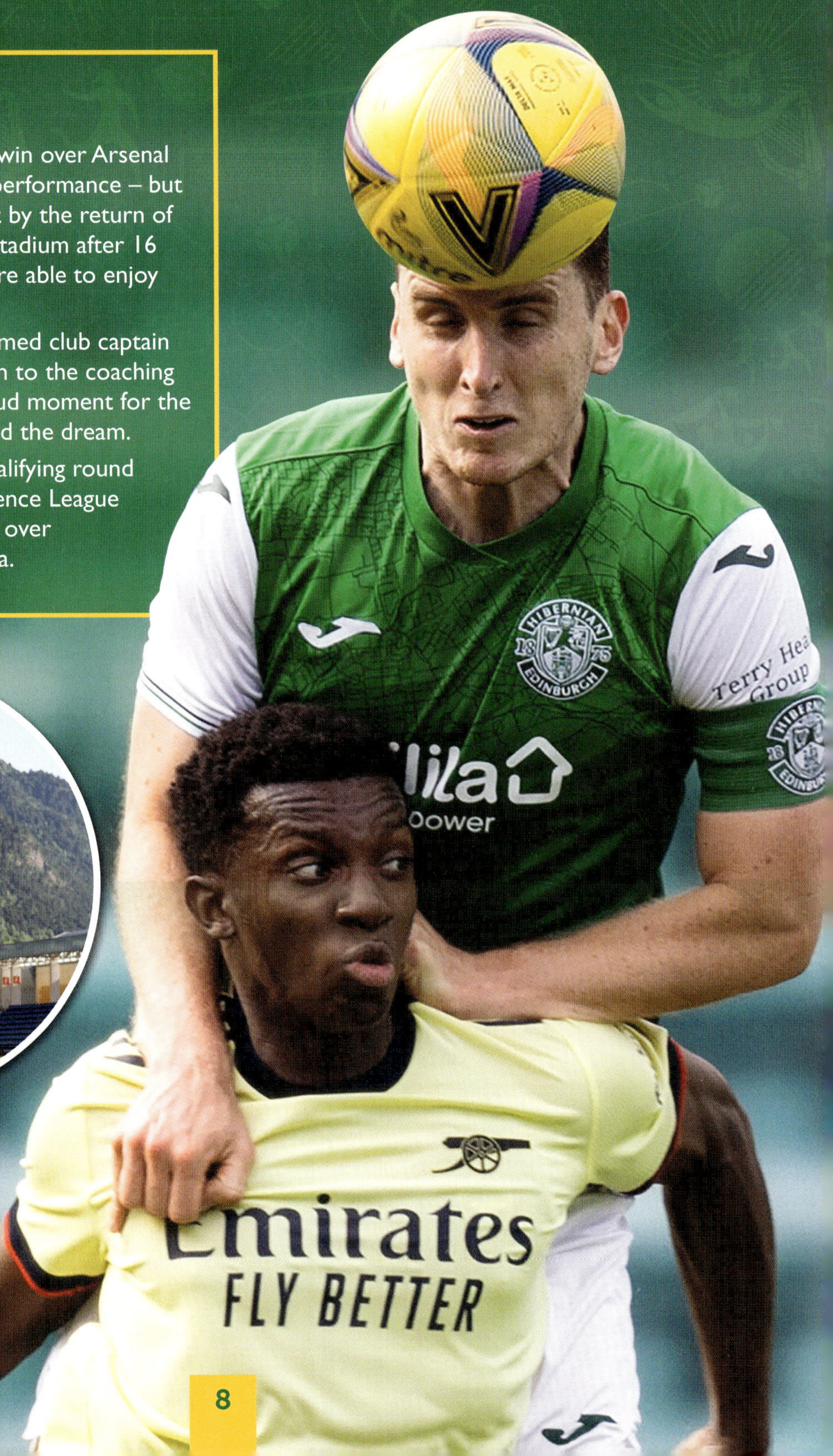

AUGUST

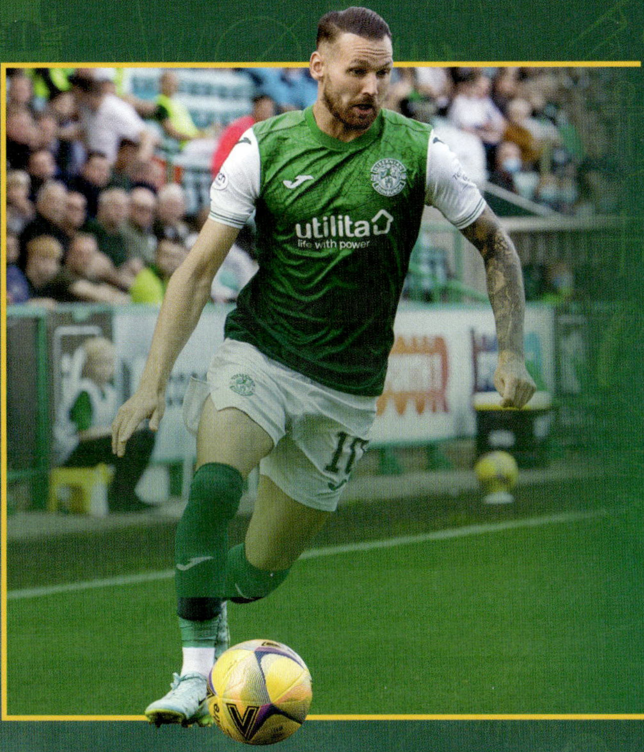

Hibs kicked off the Premiership season with a hard-fought 3-2 win at Motherwell, with Kyle Magennis, Christian Doidge and Martin Boyle all on target.

The Hibees were edged out of European competition by Croatians HNK Rijeka over two legs, either side of an impressive 3-0 defeat of Ross County at Easter Road.

Talisman Martin Boyle delivered some great news by putting pen to paper on an extended contract through until the summer of 2024.

Ryan Porteous also had cause for celebration, as he made his 100th appearance for the club in the 2-0 win over Livingston.

SEPTEMBER

Paul McGinn won his first cap as a senior Scotland player in the important 1-0 away win in Austria that helped maintain momentum for Steve Clarke's side in their World Cup qualification campaign. He lined up alongside brother – and former Hibee – John McGinn.

Martin Boyle was named the Premiership's Player of the Month for August, having scored four goals from his first four league games – the first Hibee to enjoy a prolific start to a top-flight campaign like that since Jim Scott in 1964-65.

A 3-1 win at Dundee United sent Hibs into the League Cup semi-finals.

Easter Road played host to Hibernian Women's 3-0 Edinburgh Derby win over Hearts – in front of a record crowd of 5,512 spectators.

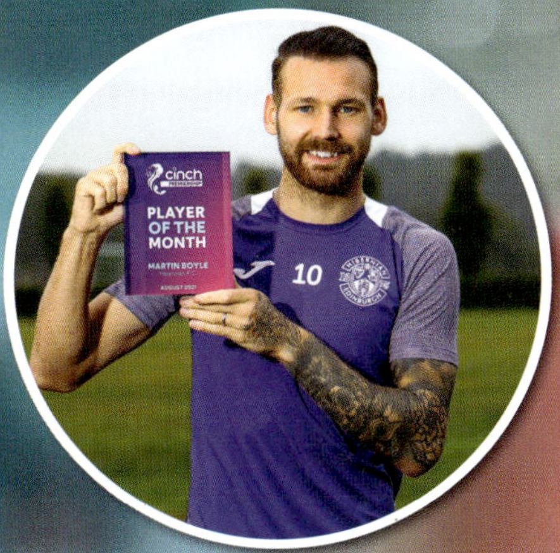

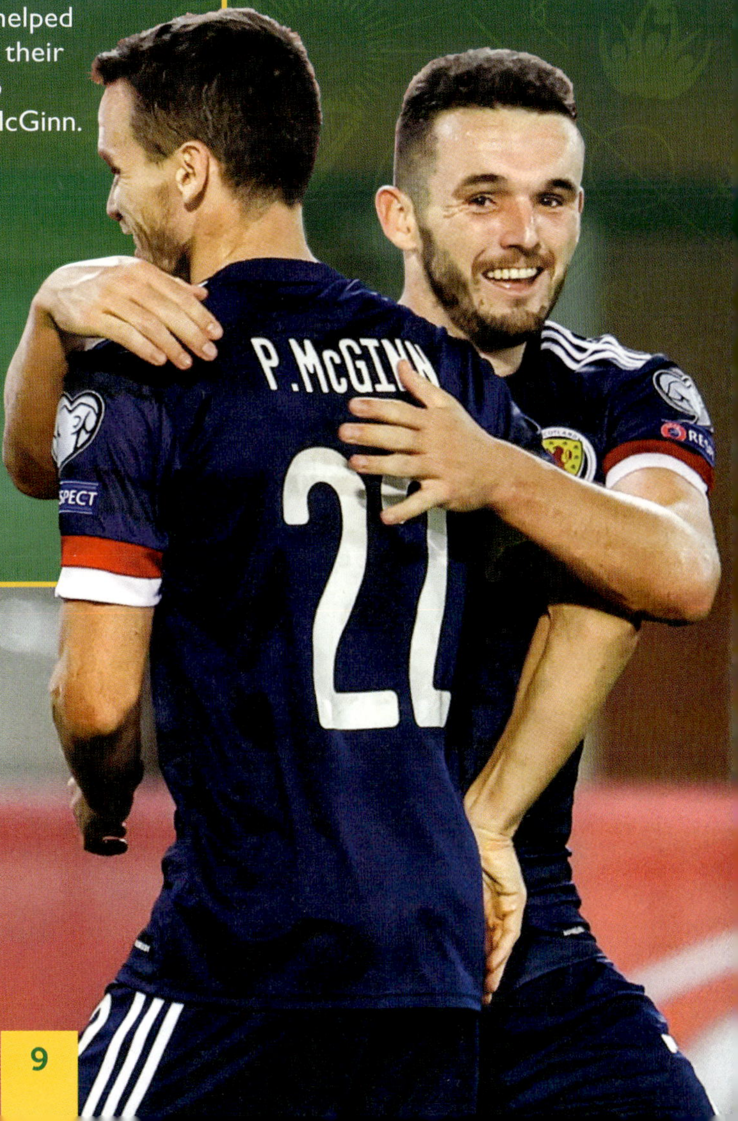

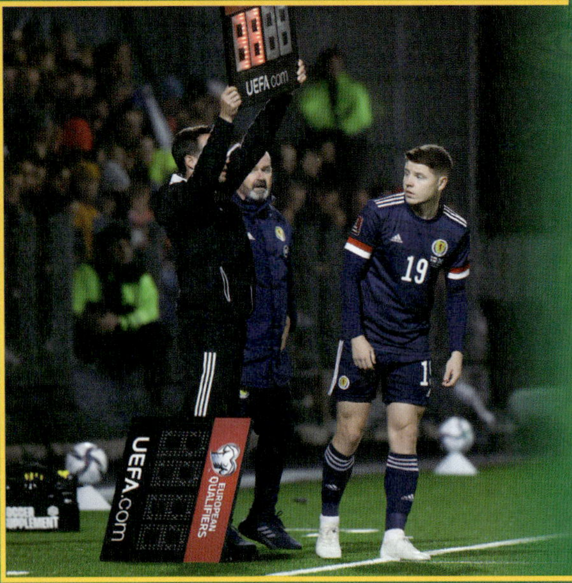

OCTOBER

Nine Hibs players were called up for action during the second international break of the season.

Kevin Nisbet was named in the Scotland squad for a double-header against Israel and Faroe Islands.

Josh Doig and James Scott were included in the Scotland Under-21 squad, Murray Johnson was with the Under-19s, while Jacob MacIntyre and Rudi Allan Molotnikov joined the Victory Shield group.

Martin Boyle joined Australia for their games against Oman and Japan, while Alex Gogic and Nathan Wood were called up by Cyprus and England's Under-20s respectively.

NOVEMBER

Captain Paul Hanlon was rewarded with an extended contract until the summer of 2024, with Lewis Stevenson signing on until 2023.

There was a new face in Steve Kean, who took up the post of Academy Director and said: "I'm convinced that player talent exists in Scotland that could quickly and effectively be developed through a programme of innovative coaching. This will provide a sustainable pool of talented players for the first team here at Hibernian FC."

Arguably, the standout highlight of the season came in the 3-1 win over Rangers at Hampden as The Hibees booked a League Cup Final place – with Martin Boyle's hat-trick the difference between the sides.

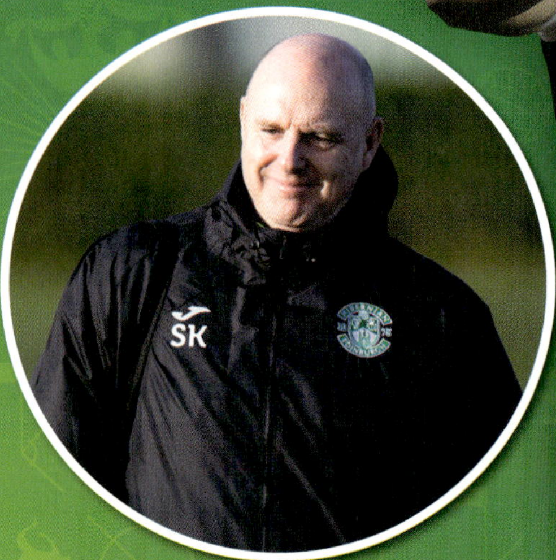

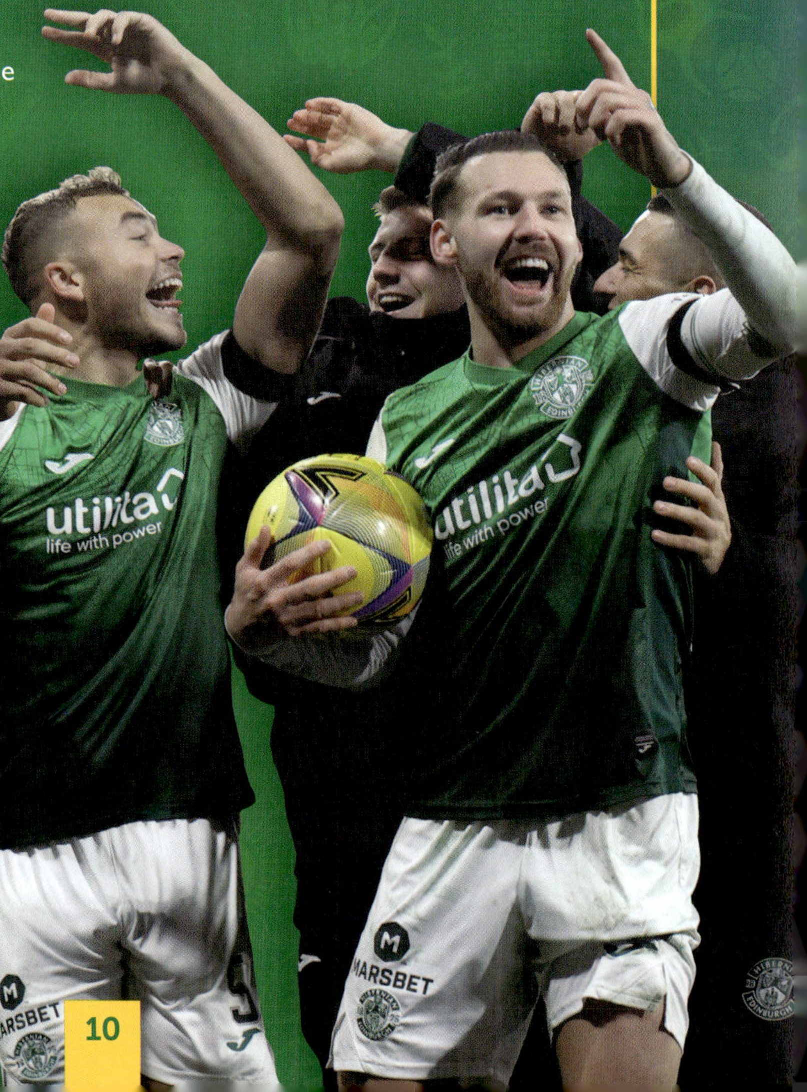

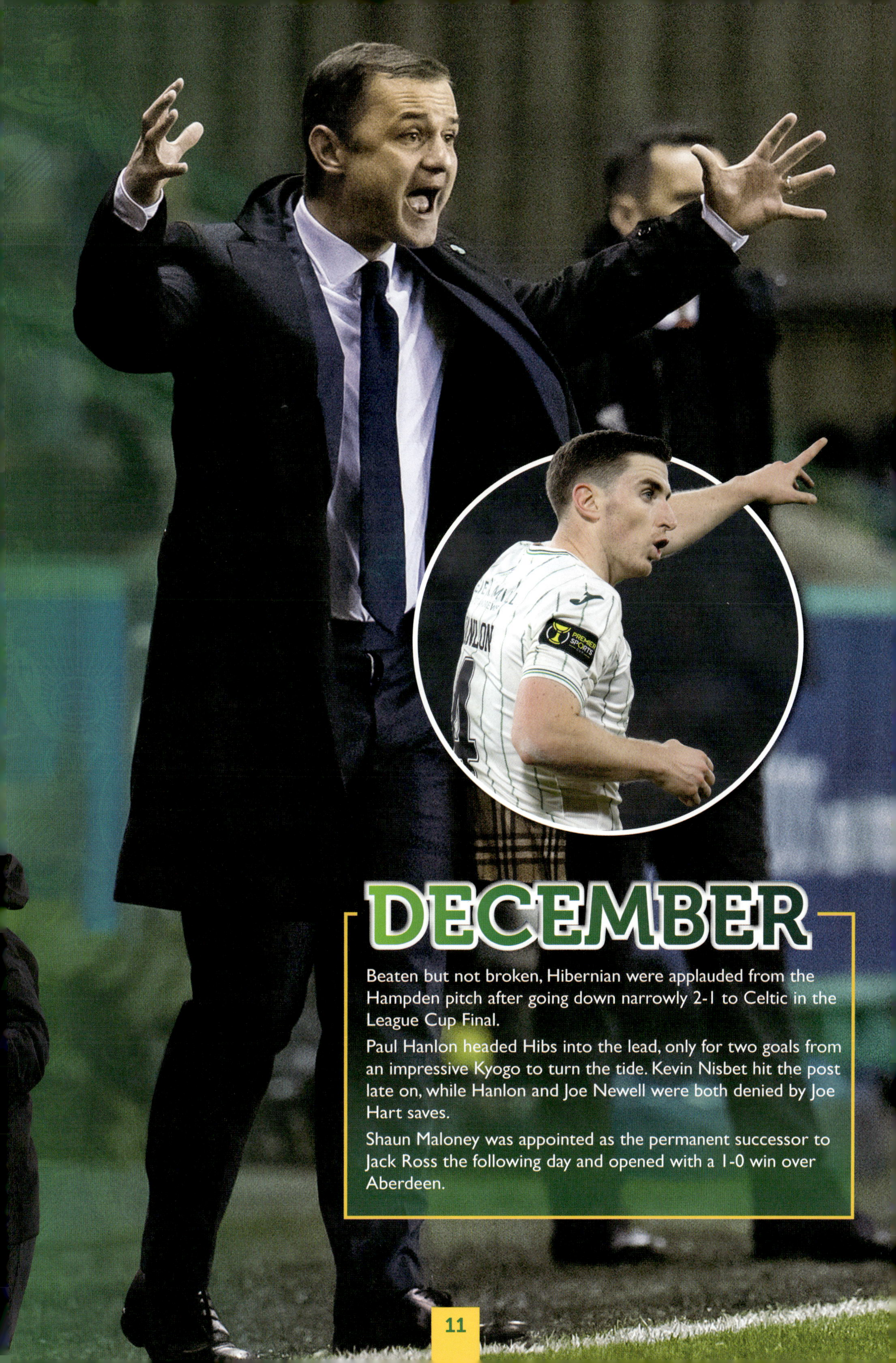

DECEMBER

Beaten but not broken, Hibernian were applauded from the Hampden pitch after going down narrowly 2-1 to Celtic in the League Cup Final.

Paul Hanlon headed Hibs into the lead, only for two goals from an impressive Kyogo to turn the tide. Kevin Nisbet hit the post late on, while Hanlon and Joe Newell were both denied by Joe Hart saves.

Shaun Maloney was appointed as the permanent successor to Jack Ross the following day and opened with a 1-0 win over Aberdeen.

JANUARY

It was a busy month at the club, with a host of new faces arriving in the transfer window.

Norwegian youth international Elias Melkersen captured the imagination on his arrival from FK Bodø/Glimt on a long-term contract.

Ewan Henderson arrived on an initial loan from Celtic, following in the footsteps of his fan favourite brother Liam.

Chris Mueller completed his move from Orlando City and was joined by Demetri Mitchell, Rocky Bushiri (on loan from Norwich City) and Sylvester Jasper (on loan from Fulham).

Going in the other direction was Martin Boyle. With a heavy heart, he put pen to paper on a switch to Saudi Arabian club Al-Faisaly.

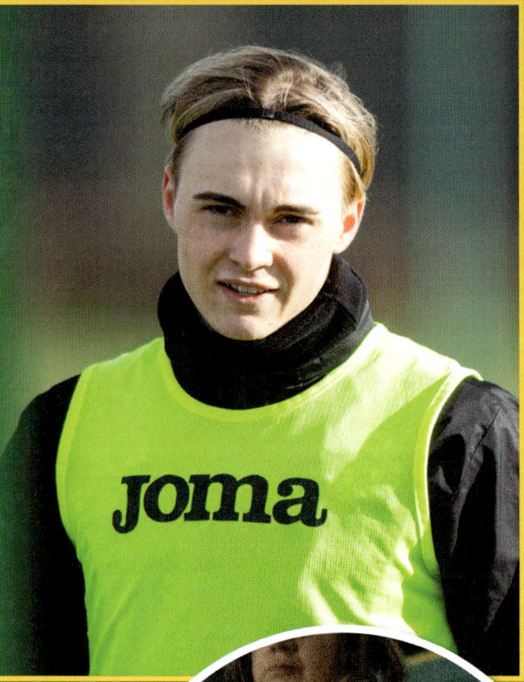

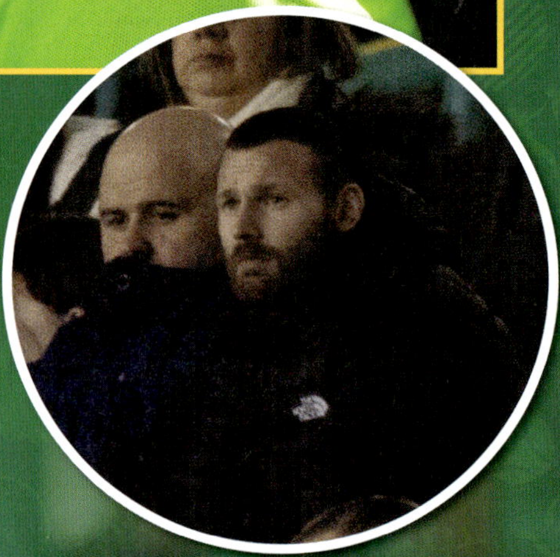

FEBRUARY

Hibs reached the last eight of the Scottish Cup after a convincing 3-1 win at Arbroath.

Craig Wighton fired the Angus men ahead, but Demetri Mitchell levelled before Kevin Nisbet and Chris Mueller rounded off the scoring.

Jake Doyle-Hayes scored his first goals for the club in a 2-0 home win over Ross County, with one of them later named Goal of the Season in the club's in-house Player of the Year awards.

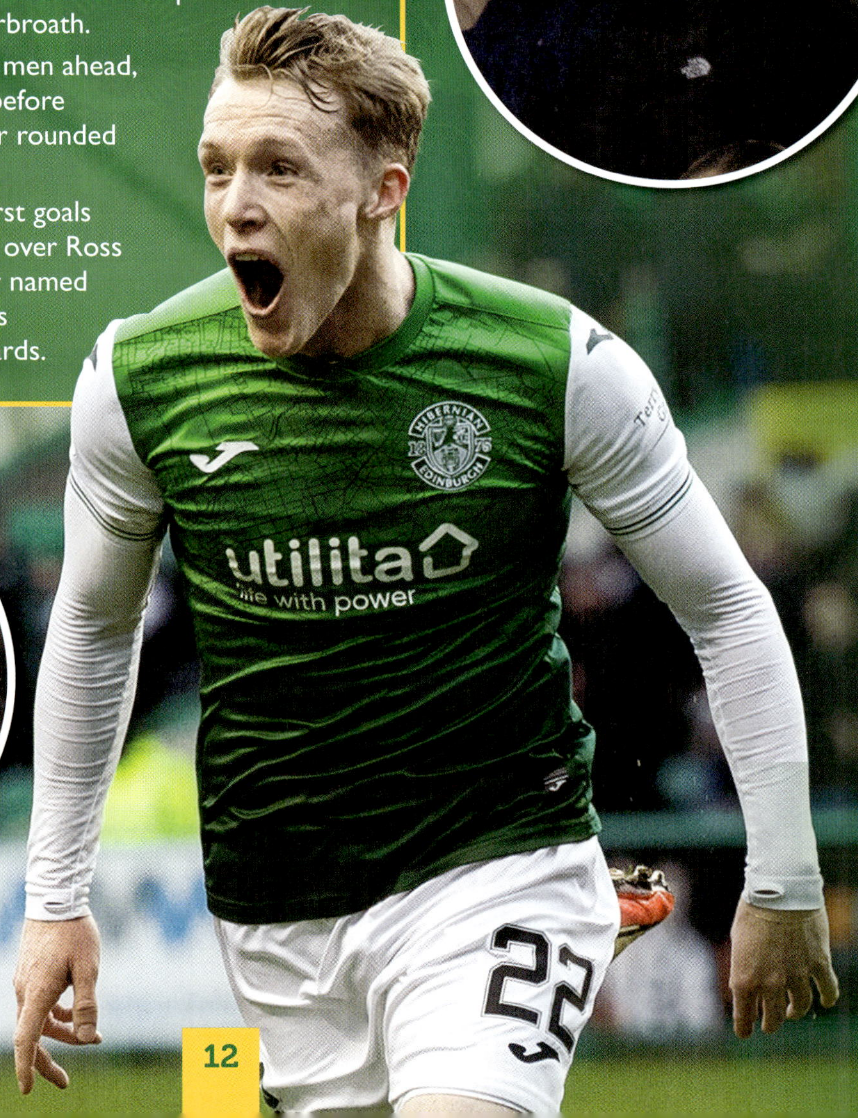

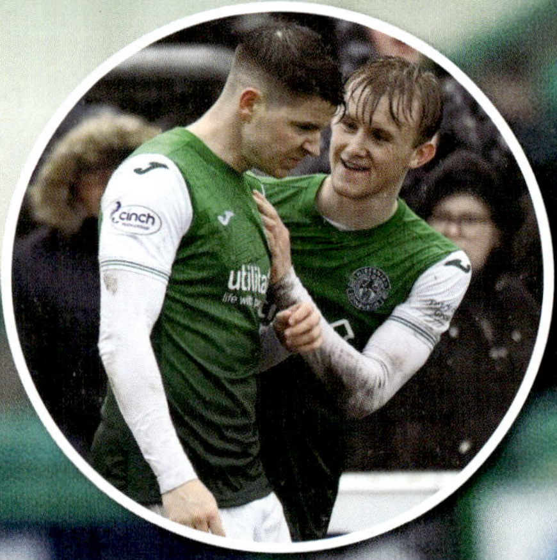

MARCH

Josh Campbell was rewarded with a first Scotland Under-21 call-up, while Elias Melkersen celebrated another first.

The striker got off the mark for Hibs with a double in his first start – a 2-1 win at Motherwell to secure a Scottish Cup semi-final appearance.

Hibernian Women showed their solidarity with the people of Ukraine by taking to the pitch in a specially adapted blue and yellow 'Hibs' kit to reflect the colours of their flag, with all proceeds of a fundraiser going to the dedicated team at Dnipro Kids.

Six legends were inducted into the Hibernian Hall of Fame at an official presentation night at Easter Road. Bobby Combe, John Blackley, Tommy Younger, Laura Kennedy, Gordon Hunter and Franck Sauzée all had their outstanding contributions to the club marked in style.

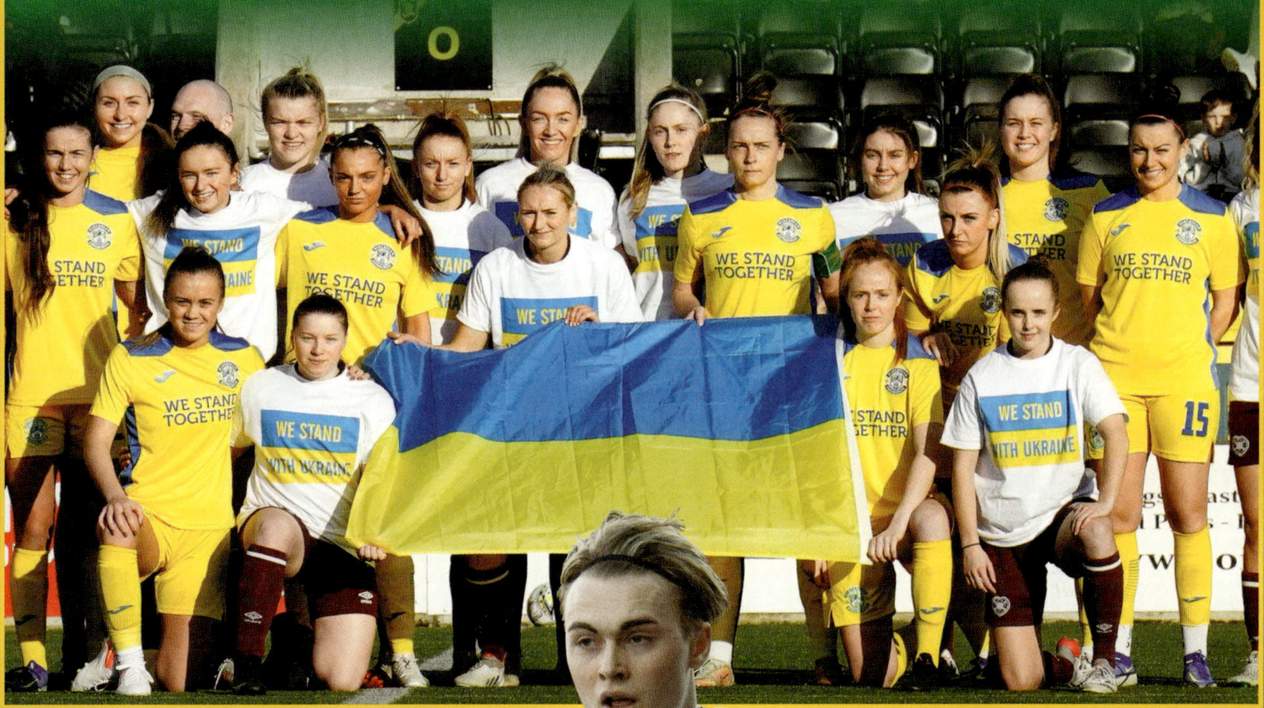

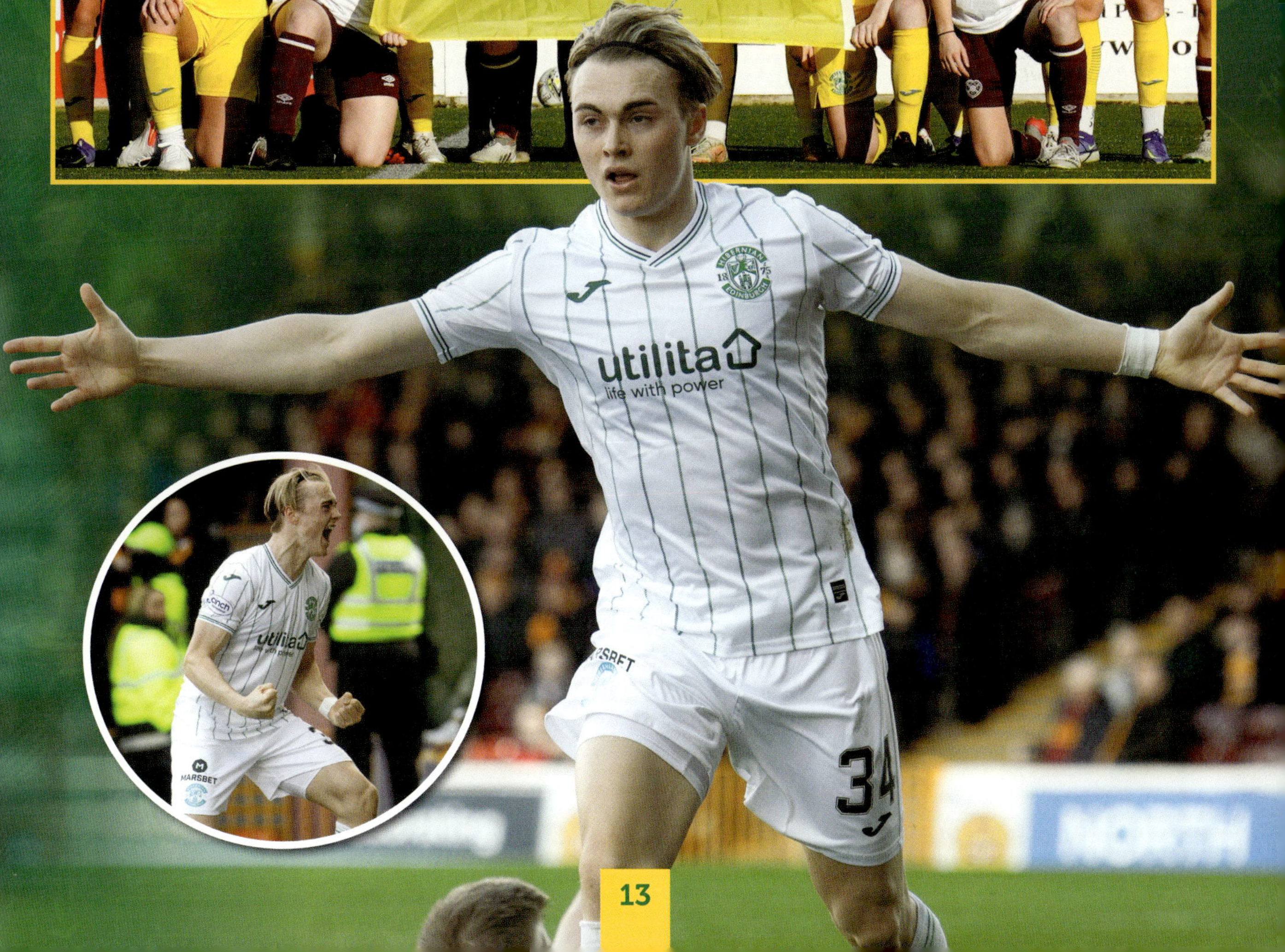

APRIL

Midfielder Joe Newell agreed a contract extension that will run until the summer of 2025.

Defender Harry Clarke – who joined on loan from Arsenal in January – was finally able to make his debut after shaking off injury and scored in a 1-1 draw with Dundee Utd at Easter Road.

A 2-1 defeat in the Scottish Cup semi-final against Heart of Midlothian was followed by the departure of Shaun Maloney, with caretaker David Gray guiding Hibs to a 1-0 win at St Mirren – which featured Ewan Henderson's first goal for the club.

Josh Doig picked up a nomination for the PFA Scotland Young Player of the Year award, while Hibernian Women captain Joelle Murray agreed an extended contract.

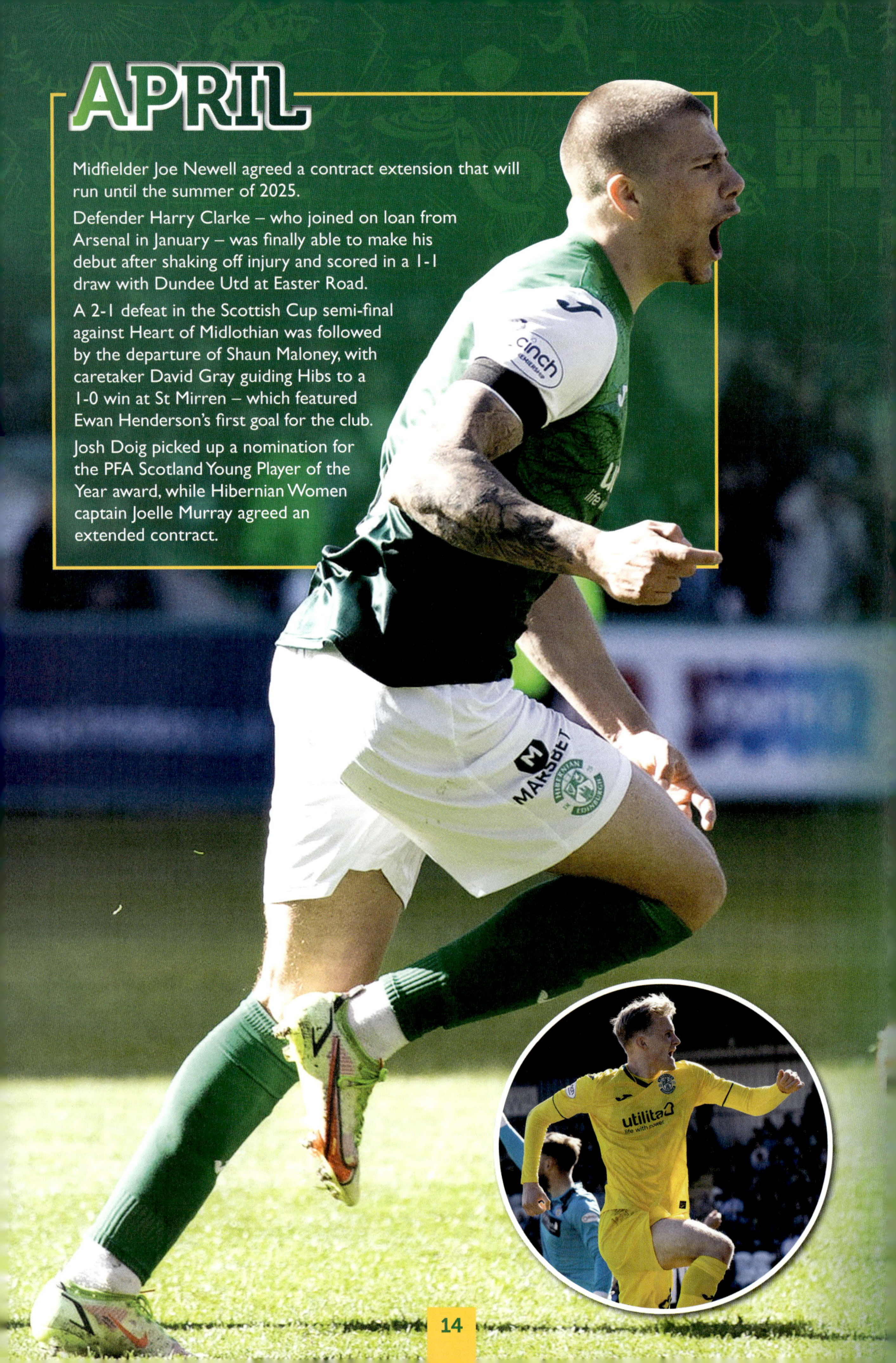

MAY

Hibs brought the curtain down on the season with a 4-0 home win over St Johnstone.

Paul McGinn opened the scoring before James Scott hit a hat-trick to clinch the biggest winning margin of the season.

Later that evening, the club held their Player of the Year awards, with Chris Cadden (Player of the Year), Ryan Porteous (Young Player of the Year), Lewis Stevenson (Players' Player of the Year), Jake Doyle-Hayes (Goal of the Season), Ellis Notley (Women's Player of the Year) and Murray Aiken (Academy Player of the Year) all honoured.

On May 19, Lee Johnson was appointed manager on a four-year contract.

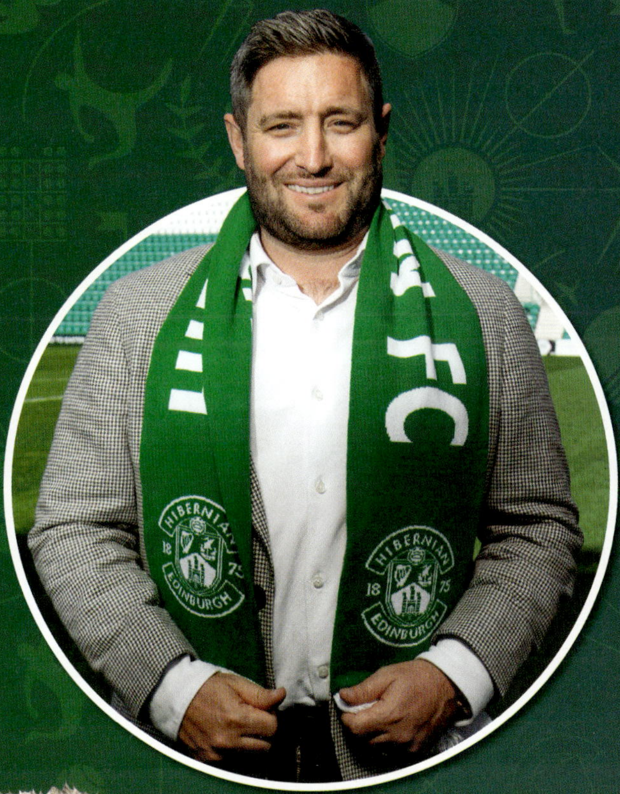

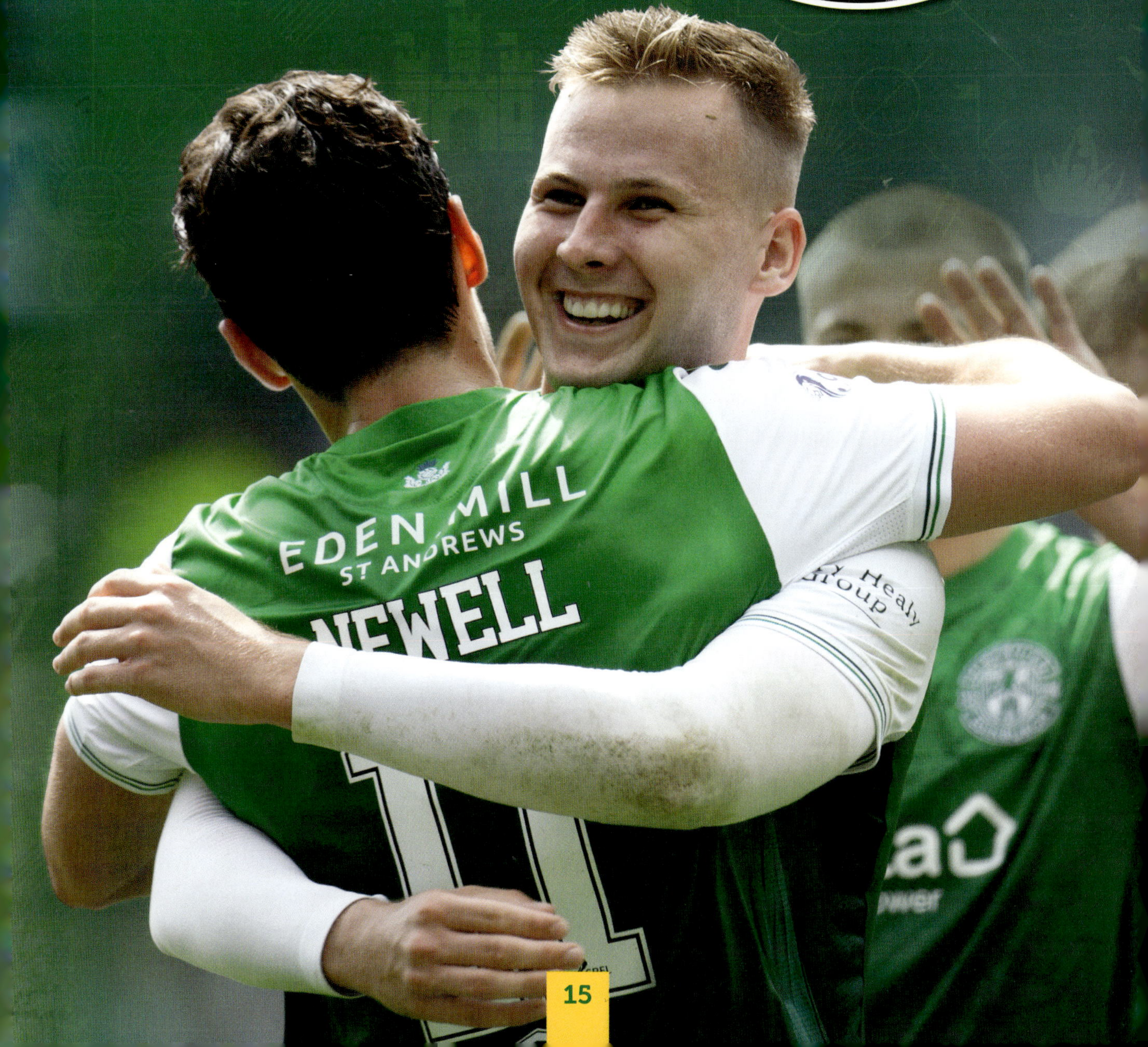

SEASON QUIZ

1. Which Andorran side did Hibernian overcome to progress to the Europa Conference League third qualifying round?

2. Who won Man of the Match on his first-team debut, against Hearts on February 1, 2022?

3. Winger Sylvester Jasper joined on loan from which English club?

4. Name the Championship club Hibs saw off to reach the last 16 of the Scottish Cup.

5. Which former Hibs midfielder assisted David Gray during his spell as caretaker manager?

6. Who was the long-serving Hibee named Players' Player of the Year?

7. Young winger Stevie Bradley impressed on loan at which club in the Republic of Ireland?

SEASON QUIZ

8. Who did Hibernian play on Paul Hanlon's 500th appearance for The Hibees?

9. Who scored a brace in the 2-1 Scottish Cup quarter-final win at Motherwell?

10. Name the player who scored a hat-trick in last November's League Cup semi-final win over Rangers.

11. Who scored Hibernian's opening goal in the 4-0 end-of-season win over St Johnstone?

12. Which two Hibees – both Academy graduates – made their Scotland Under-21 debuts in season 2021/22?

13. Who won Goal of the Season for a stunning strike against Ross County?

14. Daniel Mackay and Dylan Tait were loaned to which Championship club?

Answers on page 58.

NEW RECRUITS

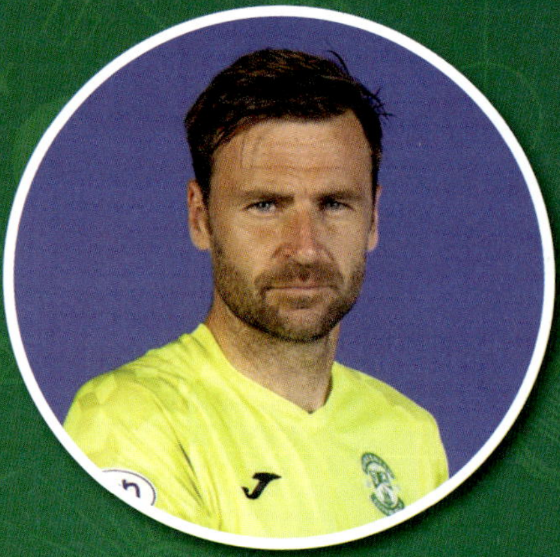

David Marshall

Veteran goalkeeper David Marshall should need little introduction. Marshall made himself a national hero with penalty shoot-out heroics against Israel and Serbia that booked Scotland's slot at Euro 2020.

With his contract up at QPR, Hibs moved quickly to tempt the former Celtic shot-stopper back north of the border – recognising what his experience and quality could add to the dressing room at Easter Road.

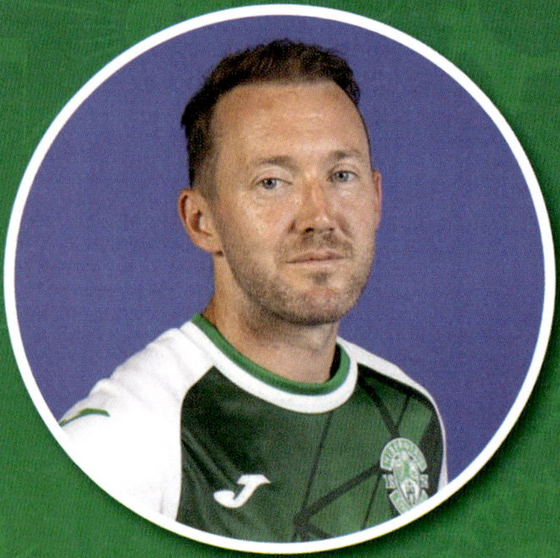

Aiden McGeady

The veteran Republic of Ireland international agreed a one-year deal to return to Scottish football and rekindle a previously successful partnership with manager Lee Johnson from Sunderland. McGeady is well known to supporters having made the breakthrough at Celtic, before subsequent spells with Spartak Moscow, Sheffield Wednesday, Preston North End and Charlton Athletic.

Most recently with The Black Cats – where he featured under Johnson – the intelligent winger was recruited to add creativity and experience to the final third.

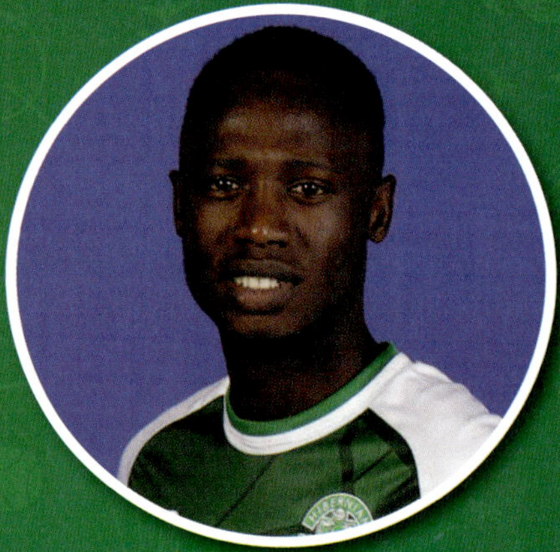

Momodou Bojang

The club sprang a surprise when they unveiled the young Gambian striker on a season-long loan move from Rainbow FC. Described as 'a pacey, direct striker with an eye for goal', Bojang has some experience of European football after a similar loan switch to Famalicao in Portugal.

Able to play as a central option or either side of a front three, Bojang is keen to impress and complete a permanent transfer.

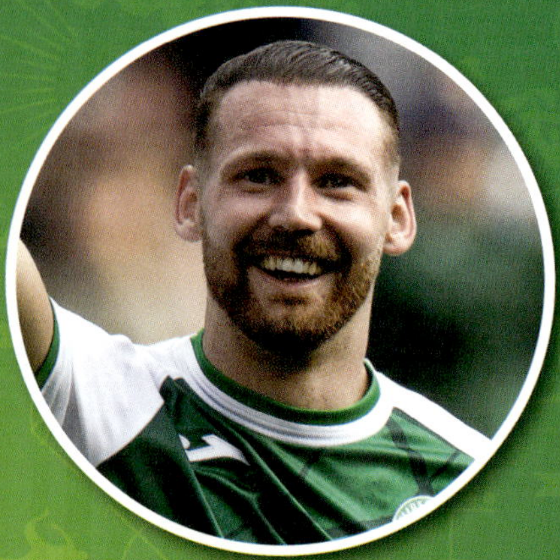

Martin Boyle

It's hard to imagine Hibs making a more popular move than sealing the return of fan favourite Martin Boyle from Saudi Arabian side Al-Faisaly. The Australian international made a point of saying it was a case of 'see you later' rather than 'goodbye' when he left Easter Road in January, but few could have predicted his return to Leith would happen so soon.

Social media was abuzz, with the winger's off-field persona as electric as his on-pitch form - typified by The Starman's Box Office introduction.

Thrown on in the Edinburgh Derby, he snatched a last-minute leveller against Hearts - sparking wild scenes of celebrations as he beat the club crest on his shirt.

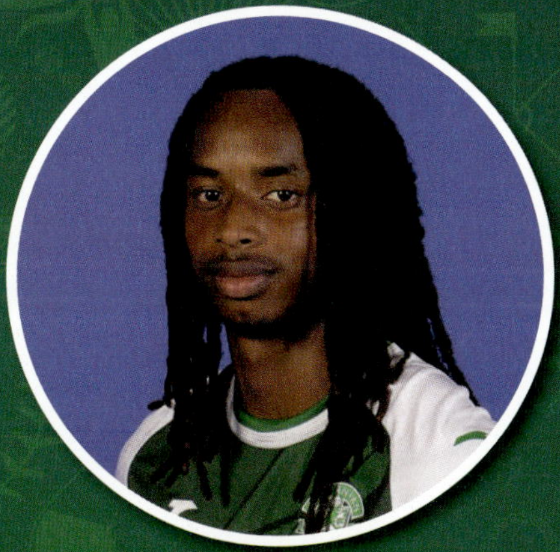

Jair Tavares

The signing of the Portuguese youth international winger may have taken most people by surprise, but manager Lee Johnson had been monitoring him since his days in England. The Benfica academy graduate agreed a contract that will run until the summer of 2026 and is known for his pace and trickery.

Tavares – who has been capped at Under-15 to Under-19 level by his country – is the cousin of Portuguese international Renato Sanches.

Lewis Miller

The signing of the Australian Under-23 international from MacArthur FC was seen as something of a coup. His form for Central Coast Mariners earned him a place in the A-League's Team of the Season.

A rampaging right-back – who is equally comfortable on the left-hand side of defence – he is highly regarded for both his technique and his tenacity.

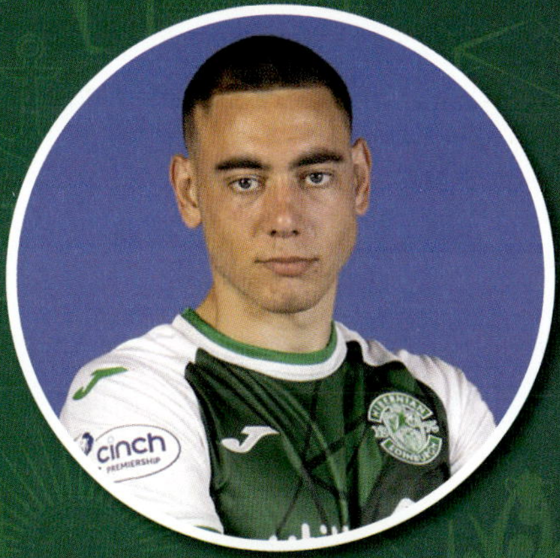

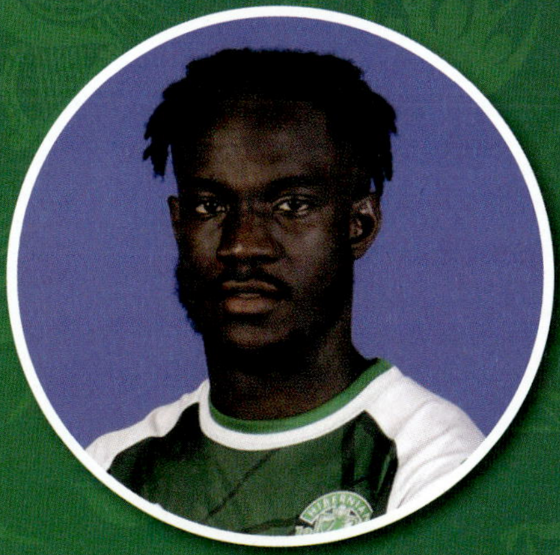

Elie Youan

The French forward arrived on loan from Swiss side St Gallen just in time for the club's pre-season trip to Portugal. The far-travelled front-man has played in his native France, Switzerland and Belgium, while he has been capped at Under-18, Under-19 and Under-20 level for his country.

Upon signing, he was described as 'a young striker who will look to stretch teams with his natural pace, who gives Lee Johnson another option to use, up front or on the left-hand-side of a front three'.

Marijan Čabraja

July 13 was a bittersweet day for Hibernian supporters, with Croatian left-back Marijan Čabraja unveiled almost as soon as popular homegrown talent Josh Doig had completed a move to Hellas Verona. The attack-minded recruit from Dinamo Zagreb has represented his country at every age level from Under-14s to Under-21s.

A loan stint with Ferencváros brought him into contact with former Hibee Adam Bogdan, who raved about life at Easter Road.

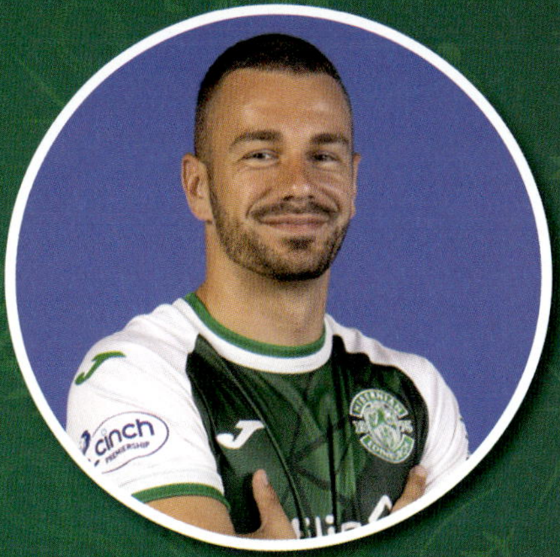

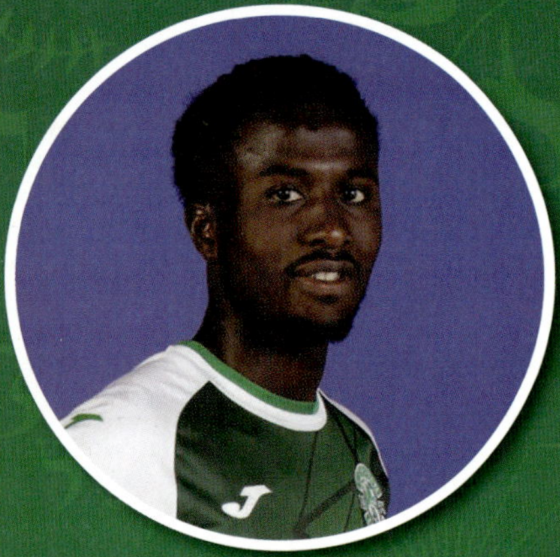

Nohan Kenneh

Hibs fought off stiff competition to snap up this versatile powerhouse from Leeds United, who were keen to keep him at Elland Road.

Kenneh made their Premier League matchday squad on 13 occasions, but opted for life in Leith in search of regular first-team football.

Born in Liberia, Kenneh has also been capped at Under-16 and Under-17 level by England.

Harry McKirdy

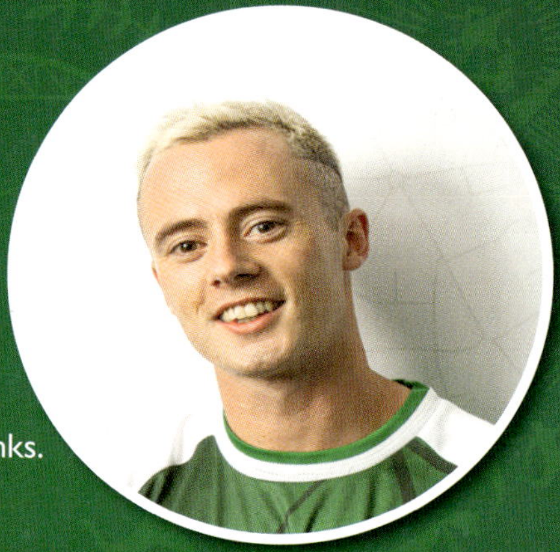

McKirdy comes to the Capital in fine form after being named in the League Two Team of the Year and the Swindon Town Player of the Year at the end of the 2021/22 campaign.

The striker bagged 23 goals in 44 games last season and carried that momentum into the current campaign scoring two in his first five matches.

The proven goalscorer is a versatile attacker, able to play centrally or on both flanks.

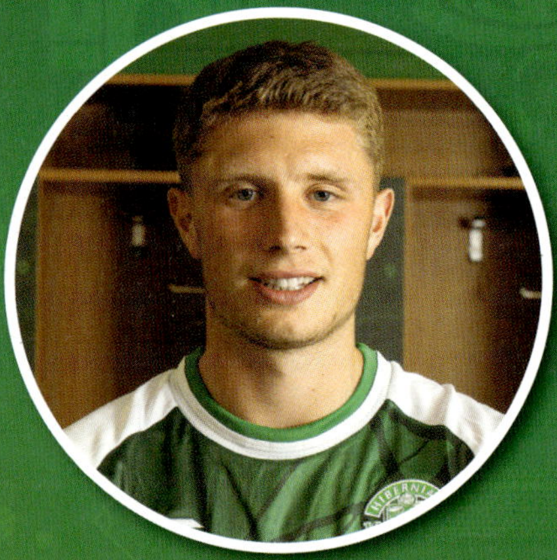

Will Fish

The highly-rated youngster spent the start of the campaign training regularly with Erik ten Hag's First Team squad and was part of Manchester United's pre-season trip to Australia.

A big, tall defender who's comfortable with the ball at his feet, Fish made his professional debut for Manchester United in May 2021 coming on as a substitute in a 2-1 win over Wolverhampton Wanderers.

His further senior appearances came on loan at Stockport County in the Vanarama National League – the fifth-tier of English football.

Alongside that, he's also been capped by England's Under-17s, U18s, and U19s and has previously played with his new team-mate Nohan Kenneh with the Three Lions youth set up.

Mykola Kukharevych

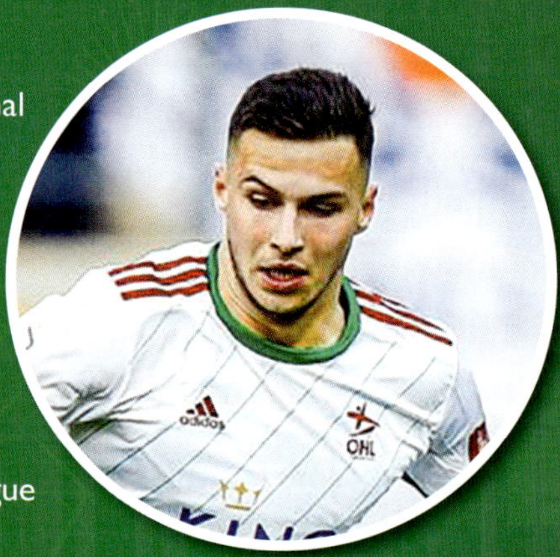

The Ukrainian U21 international will join us for the remainder of the 2022/23 campaign on loan from French Ligue 1 side ES Troyes AC, subject to international clearance and work permit approval.

ES Troyes AC joined the City Football Group in 2020 and have been working closely with Manchester City to develop the best young talent from around Europe.

After signing a long-term deal with ES Troyes AC, the 21-year-old has featured against Champions League sides like PSG and Club Brugge. Alongside this, he has spent the last 14-months on loan at Oud-Heverlee (OH) Leuven in Belgium.

The big, strong centre-forward has made four appearances in the Jupiler Pro League this season, building on from First Team minutes in the same division last season.

He has also earned 12 caps for Ukraine's Under-21s and scored three goals.

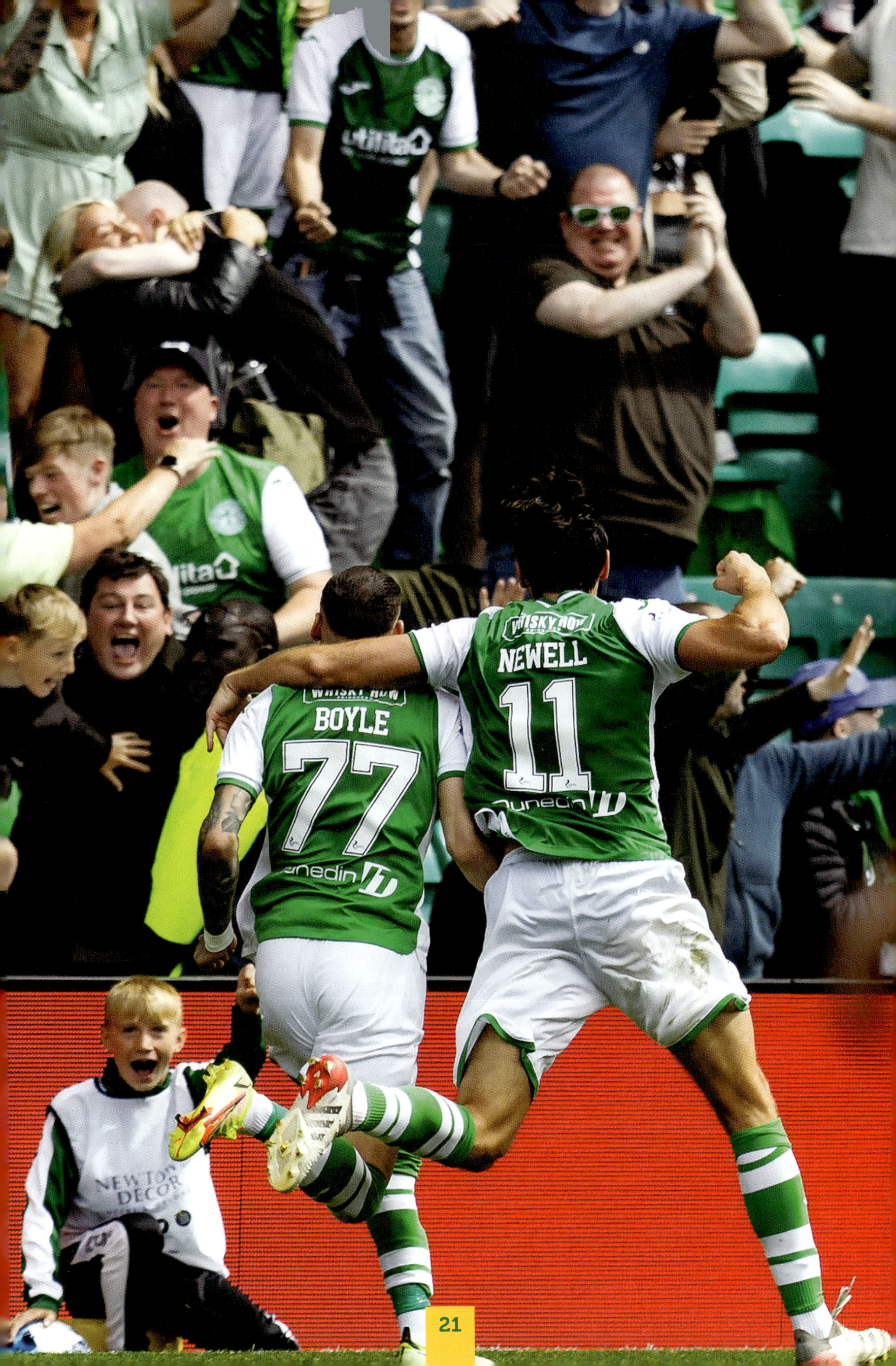
NEWELL
11
BOYLE
77

KEVIN NISBET

Kevin Nisbet is a man out to make up for lost time this season.

The Scotland striker's 2021/22 season was cruelly cut short by a tear of his anterior cruciate ligament in March – sustained in an innocuous collision with Celtic defender Carl Starfelt.

It was tough on Nisbet and the team alike, with his absence keenly felt in the remainder of the campaign.

However, it's not the first setback he's faced in a rollercoaster career and he has vowed to return stronger than ever after a gruelling rehabilitation period.

Looking back on the incident, he recalled: "I knew instantly that it was a bad one.

"I heard the pop and I felt it straight away. I think my reaction showed something was really wrong.

"Then I tried to get back up to play on, but my knee buckled and that was it.

"I hoped it was going to be a smaller injury, but it was my anterior cruciate ligament and medial collateral ligament.

"When they say that to you, then you know it's the worst case scenario. It was terrible to hear it confirmed after the scans, but I was pretty convinced before going to the appointment what was coming.

"The doctors at Hibs had done tests on me, and they said that's what they thought it was. It's still hard to hear, though, when they say 'ACL'.

"It was a tough first few days as I was in a brace and I couldn't really do anything.

"I wanted to get the operation over and done with, so I could start my recovery quickly.

"It was my first major injury, so I have been lucky. In football, I never get too high or too low. That's the way I have always been.

"I've had ups and downs off the park as well. Everyone knows what happened with my Dad.

"That was the toughest thing I've ever faced in my life. So if I could get through that, I can get

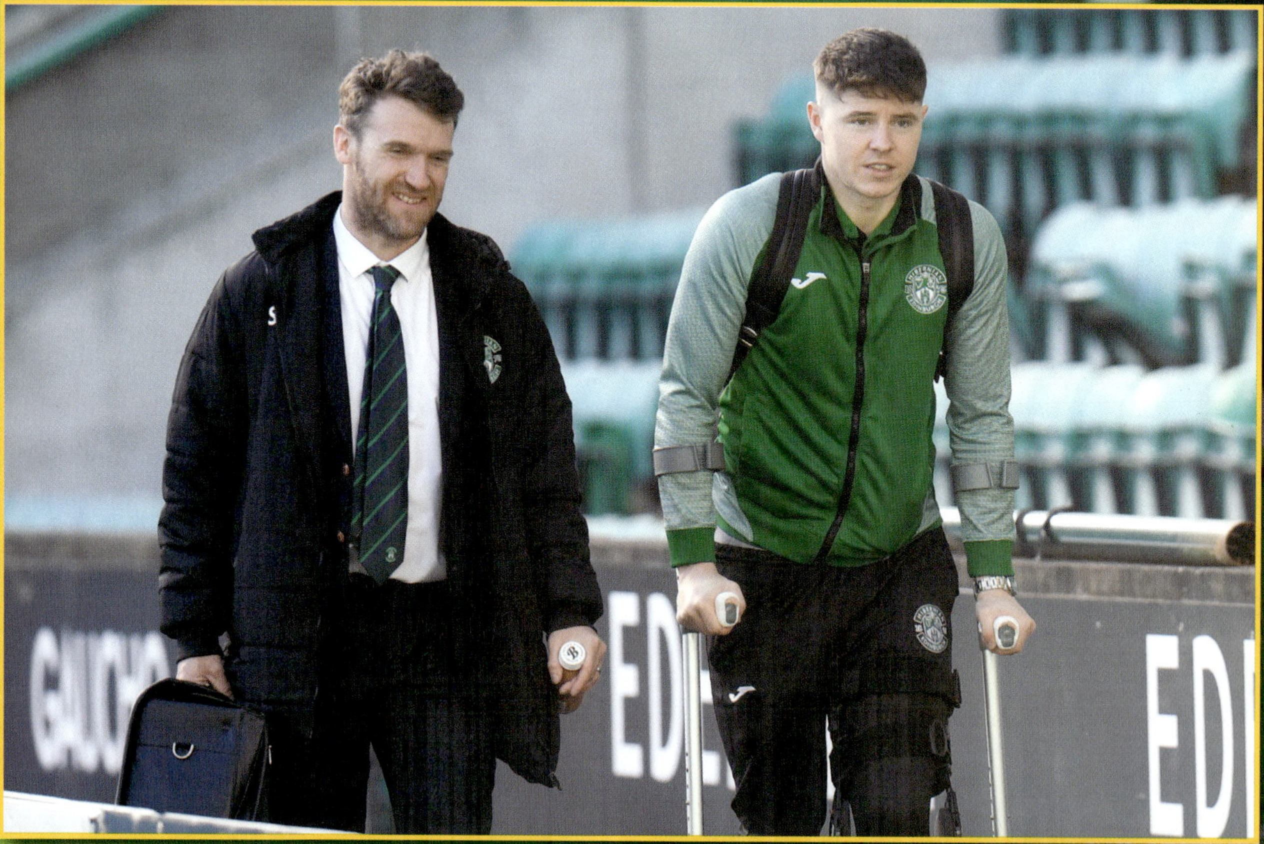

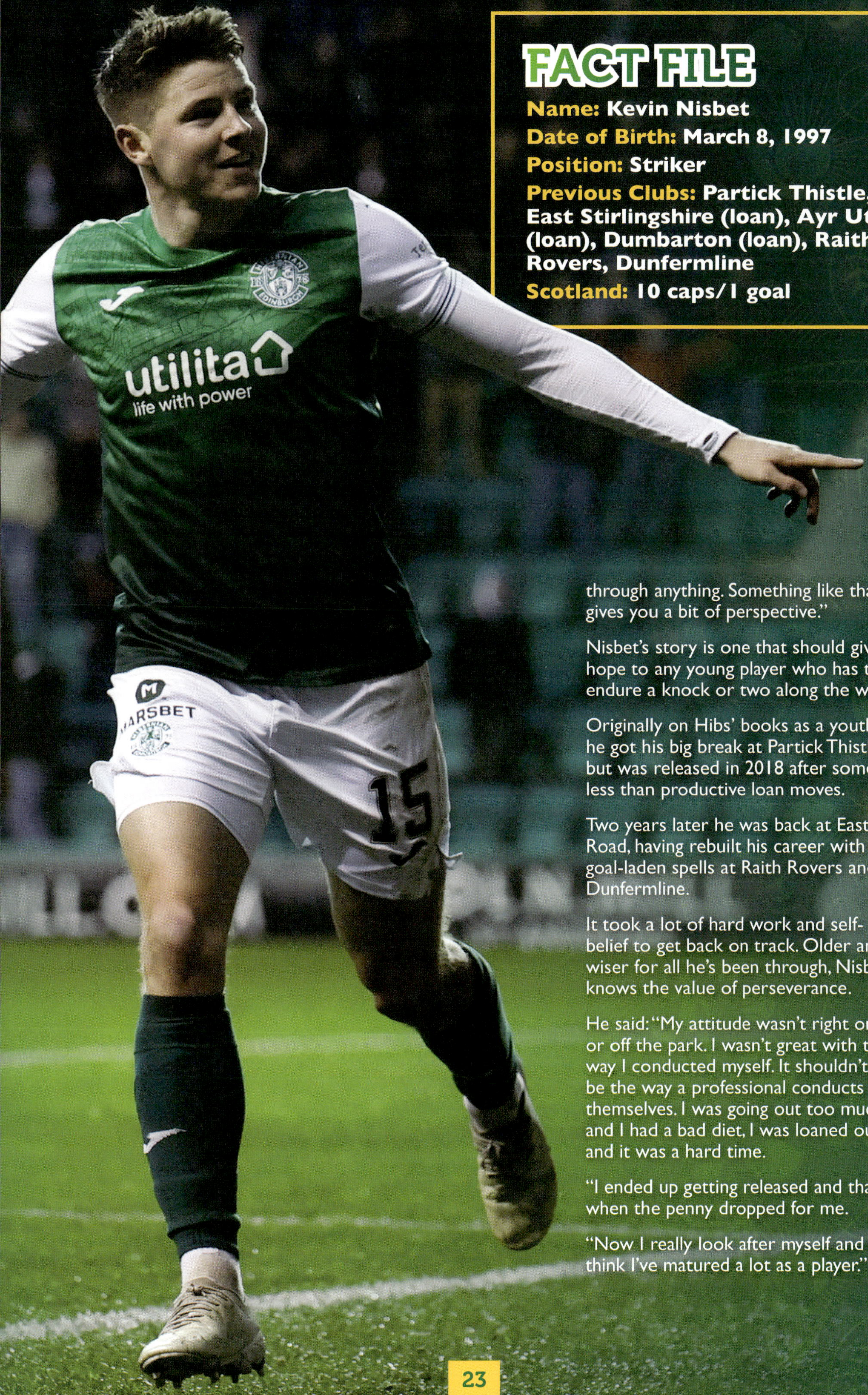

FACT FILE

Name: Kevin Nisbet
Date of Birth: March 8, 1997
Position: Striker
Previous Clubs: Partick Thistle, East Stirlingshire (loan), Ayr Utd (loan), Dumbarton (loan), Raith Rovers, Dunfermline
Scotland: 10 caps/1 goal

through anything. Something like that gives you a bit of perspective."

Nisbet's story is one that should give hope to any young player who has to endure a knock or two along the way.

Originally on Hibs' books as a youth, he got his big break at Partick Thistle but was released in 2018 after some less than productive loan moves.

Two years later he was back at Easter Road, having rebuilt his career with goal-laden spells at Raith Rovers and Dunfermline.

It took a lot of hard work and self-belief to get back on track. Older and wiser for all he's been through, Nisbet knows the value of perseverance.

He said: "My attitude wasn't right on or off the park. I wasn't great with the way I conducted myself. It shouldn't be the way a professional conducts themselves. I was going out too much and I had a bad diet, I was loaned out and it was a hard time.

"I ended up getting released and that's when the penny dropped for me.

"Now I really look after myself and I think I've matured a lot as a player."

HIBERNIAN COMMUNITY FOUNDATION

Any football club has to be about more than 11 players on a football pitch.

The Hibernian Community Foundation play a vital role in the local community and is truly something for Hibees everywhere to be proud of.

We caught up with their Chief Executive Officer, Lewis Melee, to learn a bit more about their work and hopes for the future.

Lewis, for people who don't know that much about the Hibernian Community Foundation, how would you describe the work done by you and your team?

Put simply, Hibernian Community Foundation is the official partner charity of Hibernian Football Club. We're based at Easter Road Stadium and use the power of football and the attraction of Hibernian to engage with members of the community from as young as three years old. Our activities are spread across the stadium, Hibernian Training Centre or on the ground in different areas of the community – including locations that suffer from real deprivation and others that are a bit more fortunate financially but face different challenges. What we do is hard to sum up because of the variety. It could be anything from helping young people with schoolwork to programmes around social inclusion, health and sporting opportunities like playing for a community team or enjoying after-school drop-in sessions. It's not just for Hibs fans or even football fans. We've got activities that bring people together that can impact positive changes in their lives, whether it's providing food or company. We all know the challenges we're going through as a society with food and fuel poverty, alongside the general rising cost of living. There's a lot of different ways we can support and I'd encourage anyone reading this to engage with us and see what we do, even if it's just on our website or social media platforms.

hiberniancommunityfoundation.org.uk

Hibernian Community Foundation

hiberniancommunity

hibsincommunity

Talk us through your own role at HCF.

I was appointed CEO in July 2021 and my day-to-day involves coordinating different projects and the general management of the Foundation as a whole. We're moving into a brand new space in the Famous Five stand, so I'm helping to manage that move and see how we can get the best use out of it as a community hub. There's also ongoing relationships with partners locally, nationally and on a European level to maintain and build on. As a team, we also have a wider responsibility to raise awareness of what we do and let people

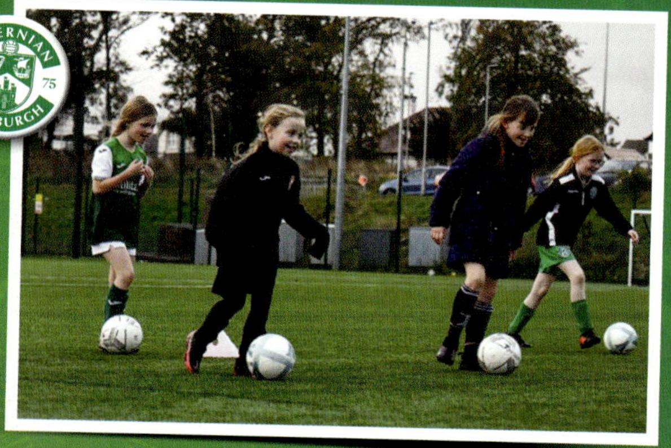

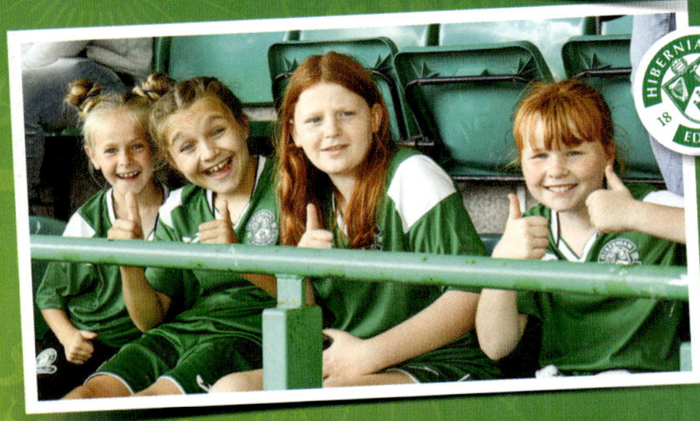

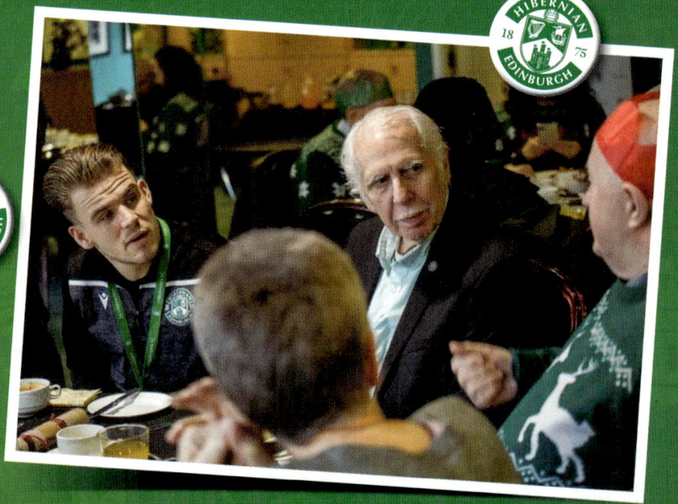

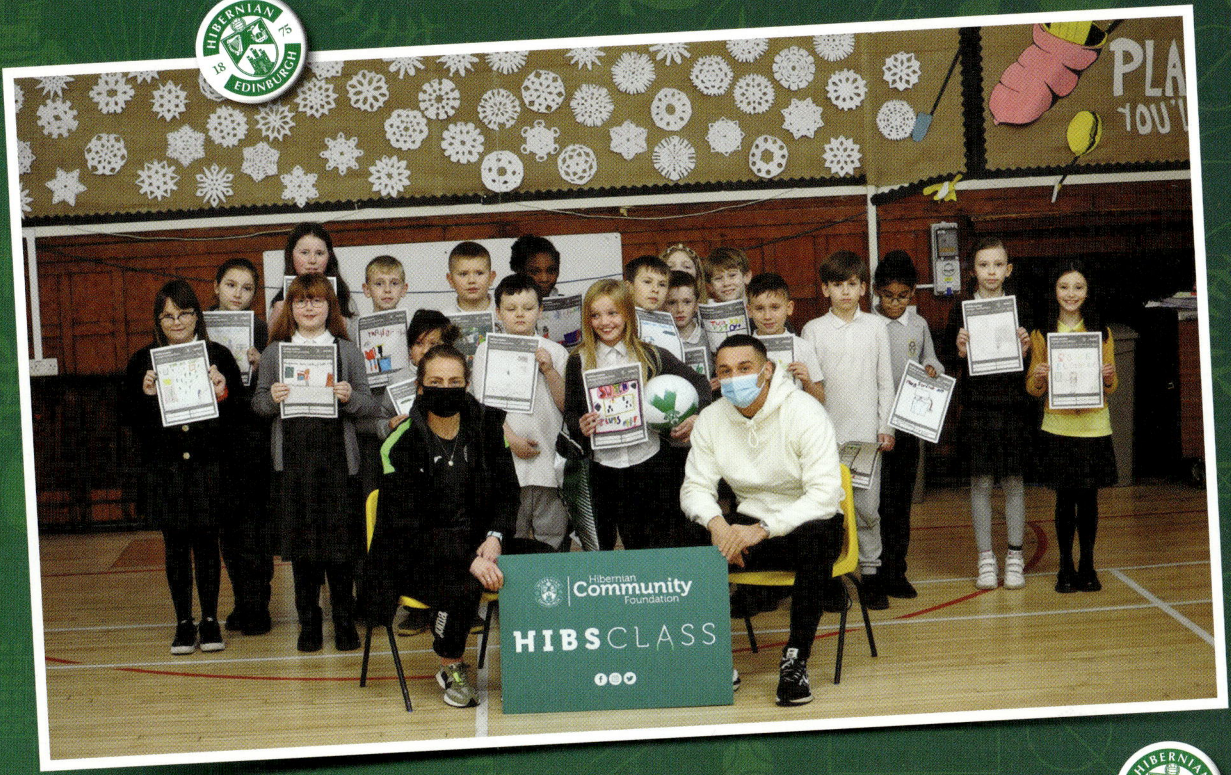

know about the opportunities that are out there for them. By their nature, football teams will have ups and downs but we're consistent in what we can offer. I like to think we have an understanding about some of the needs in our community but we can't know everything, so we also need to be constantly aware of new people and groups who could use our help.

What kind of stuff has HCF been up to in the last year?

Thankfully the world's returned to some sort of normality, so we've been able to bring a lot of activities back. Football Memories is one example of that – a social inclusion project run in partnership with the club that was hit hard by Covid. Our Monday lunch club, again, promotes inclusion and offers somewhere for people to grab a bite to eat and take a few things away with them. The Changing Room has enjoyed some good publicity for their work around mental health, while we launched Bright Sparks in schools around the idea of Hibs being 'the greenest club in Scotland'. It's a five-week education programme around things like 'reduce, reuse and recycle, our use of electricity and water and how we can look after the planet a bit better. Game On – run by my colleague, Lynsey – works with local children who are care or trauma experienced. They come to us one day a week to build skills that will help with future employment opportunities or just societal integration in general. There's always a lot going on!

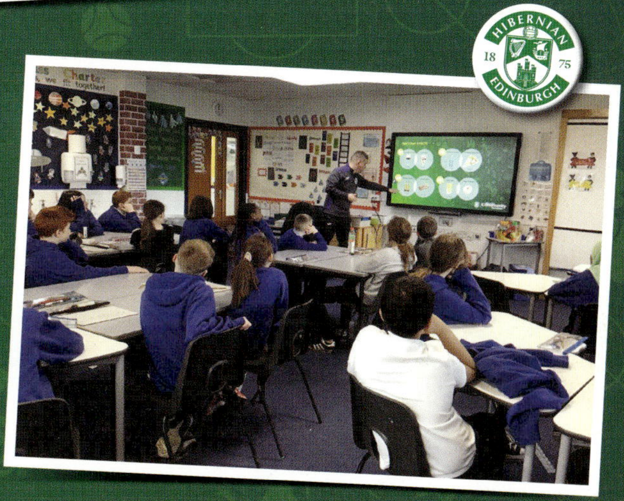

What's next?

Our new space in the Famous Five stand needs a bit of work and time spent on it. That's not going to be a quick fix, but the longer-term goal is to bring that up to scratch and make it a real hub for the community. We'd love to see an education space, a café and maybe somewhere for the local community to come and exercise. We want to maintain the outreach that we have and not let things drop, while working even more directly with the immediate community around Easter Road. If there are needs, we want to be some of the first people to respond and help. Personally speaking, I've been a Hibs supporter all my life and it fills me with pride to represent the club I love in this capacity and I know I speak for the team in that respect. We don't take anything for granted, but seeing smiles on faces and positive changes gives us real satisfaction and the encouragement to keep pushing on.

PLAYER SQUAD PROFILES

KEVIN DABROWSKI

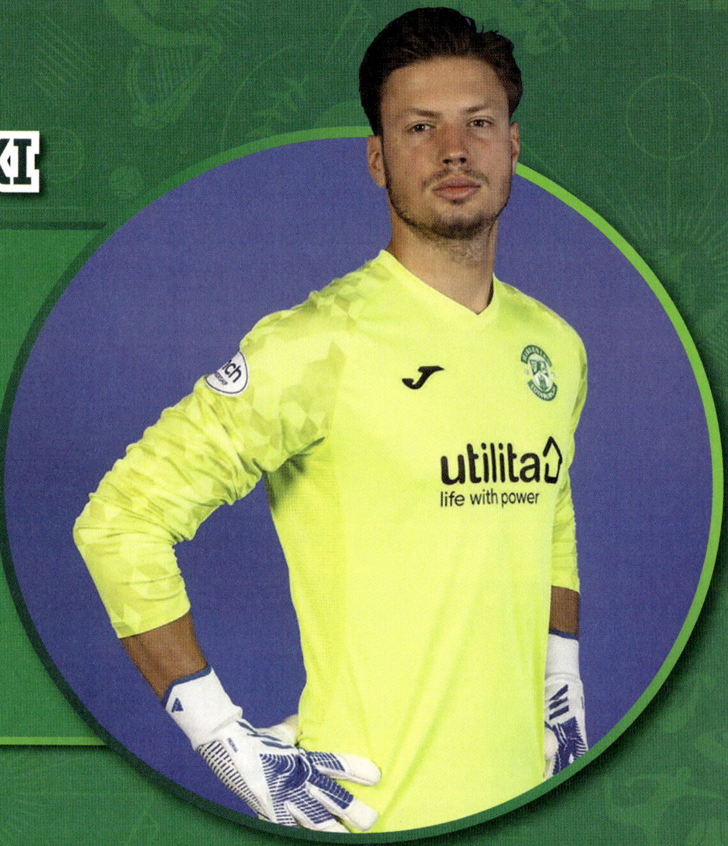

The Academy graduate is a popular figure around HTC, with a beaming smile never far from his face.

The Polish keeper had to be patient for his first-team bow, but took the opportunity when it was presented to him with a Man of the Match display against Hearts.

Dabrowski is determined to show that was no one-off and that he belongs at this level.

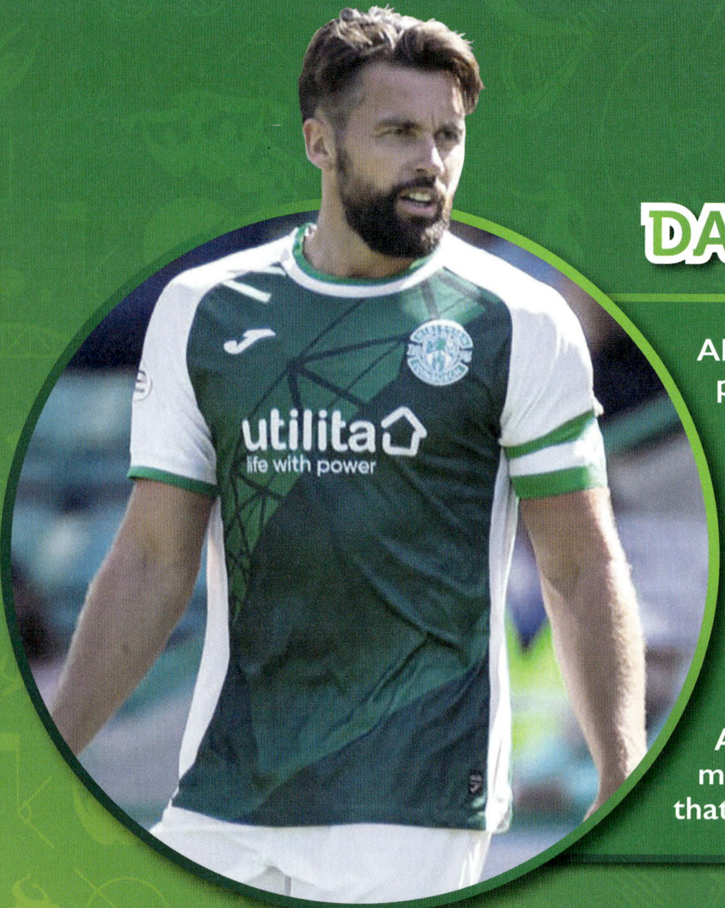

DARREN MCGREGOR

Although he's transitioned from first pick to a reliable back-up in the twilight of his career, Darren McGregor's influence at Easter Road remains invaluable.

Having knocked back offers to play more regularly elsewhere because of his love of the club, McGregor has never let The Hibees down when called upon.

A Hibs man to the core and a modern-day legend for his part in that Scottish Cup-winning team.

DEMETRI MITCHELL

Mitchell moved to Hibs in January 2022 for an undisclosed fee from Blackpool, and he made an instant impact with assists and goals either side of some frustrating niggling injuries.

Able to play on either flank – across the backline or further forward – the former Manchester United prospect gives Lee Johnson real options.

Creative and quick, Mitchell was capped at Under-20 level by England.

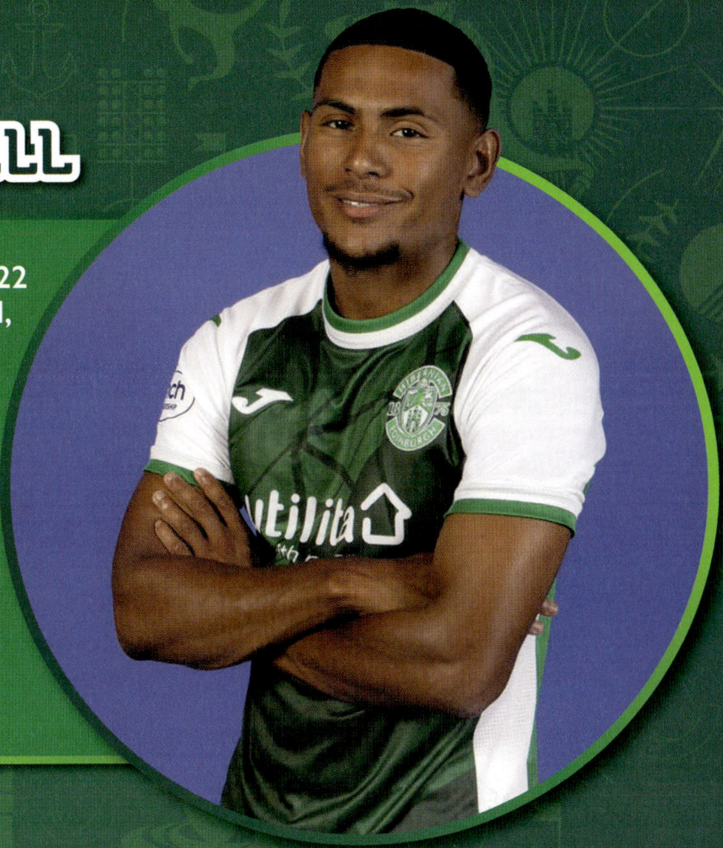

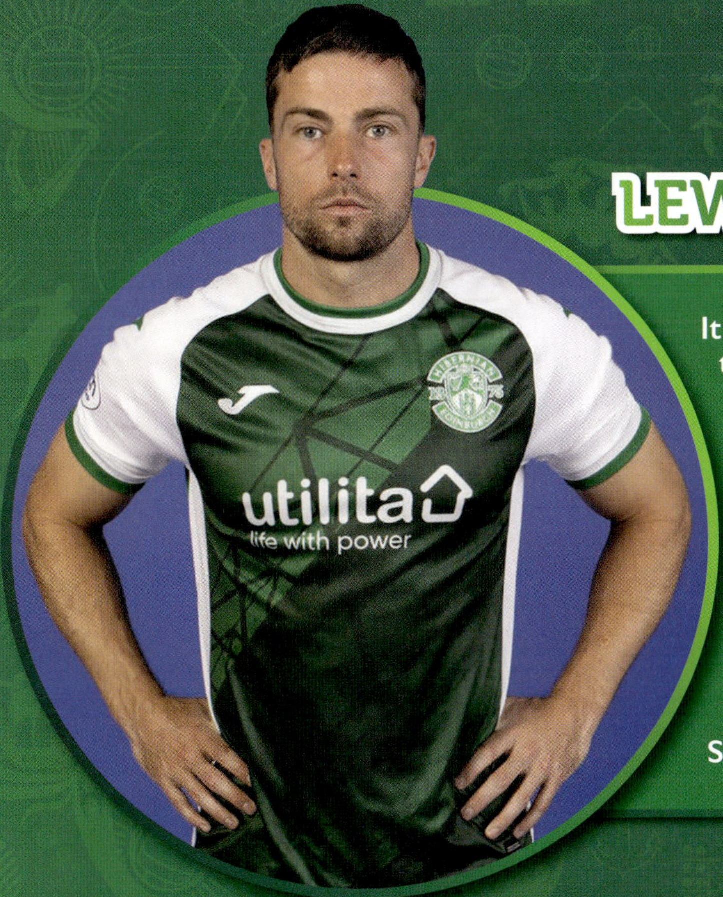

LEWIS STEVENSON

It says everything about Lewis that he turned in some of the best performances of his Hibs career last season.

Still as driven and professional as ever, he's shown himself to be as comfortable in the engine room as he is at left-back.

A legend, pure and simple, who continues to do his bit off the park as well through the Hanlon Stevenson Foundation.

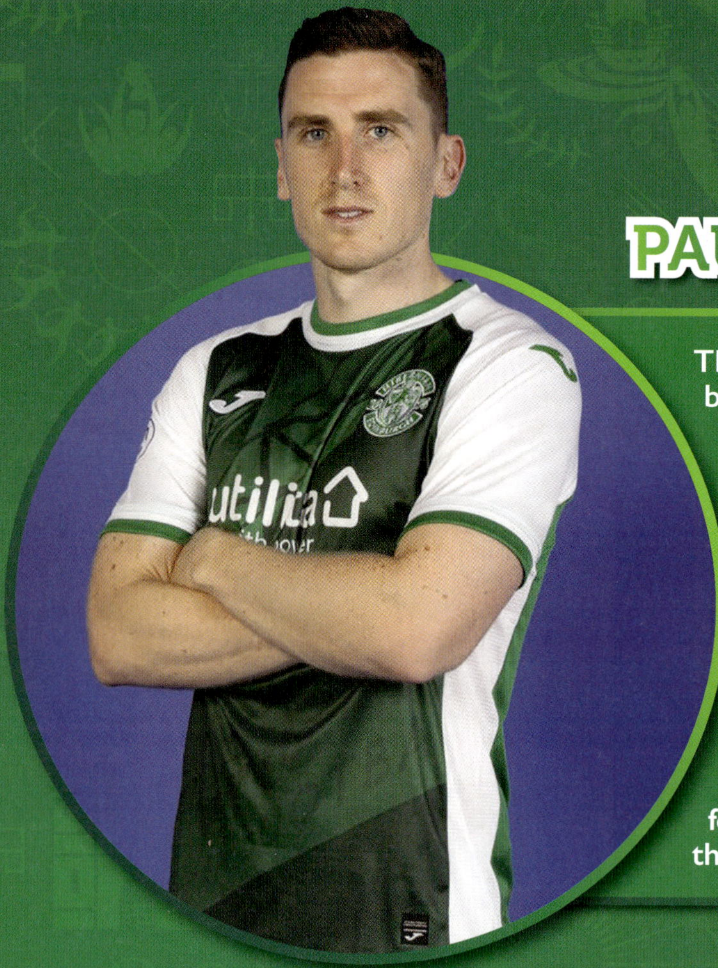

PAUL HANLON

The club captain, who continues to lead by example, and a Hibee through and through.

The boyhood Hibs supporter and Academy graduate shows no signs of slowing down, and is a calming influence in a defence that has been statistically one of the strongest in the Premiership over the last couple of seasons.

Like his long-time team-mate and friend, Lewis Stevenson, he remains a force for good in the community through the Hanlon Stevenson Foundation.

ROCKY BUSHIRI

The former Belgian Under-21 centre-back joined permanently in the summer of 2022 after a six-month loan move from Norwich City.

Hibs described him as a player of real potential, who will work hard to smooth any rough edges on his game.

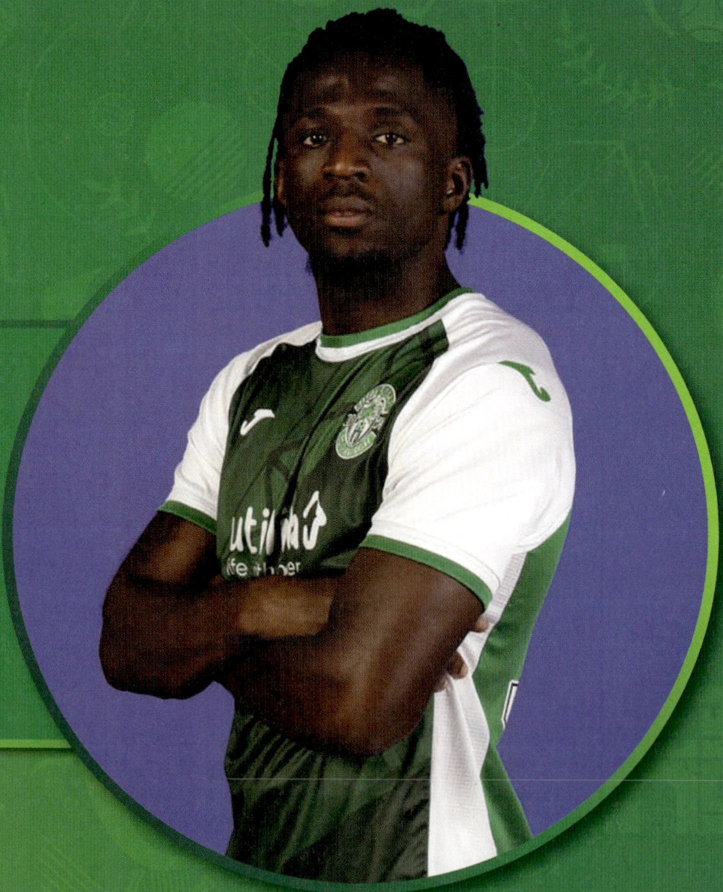

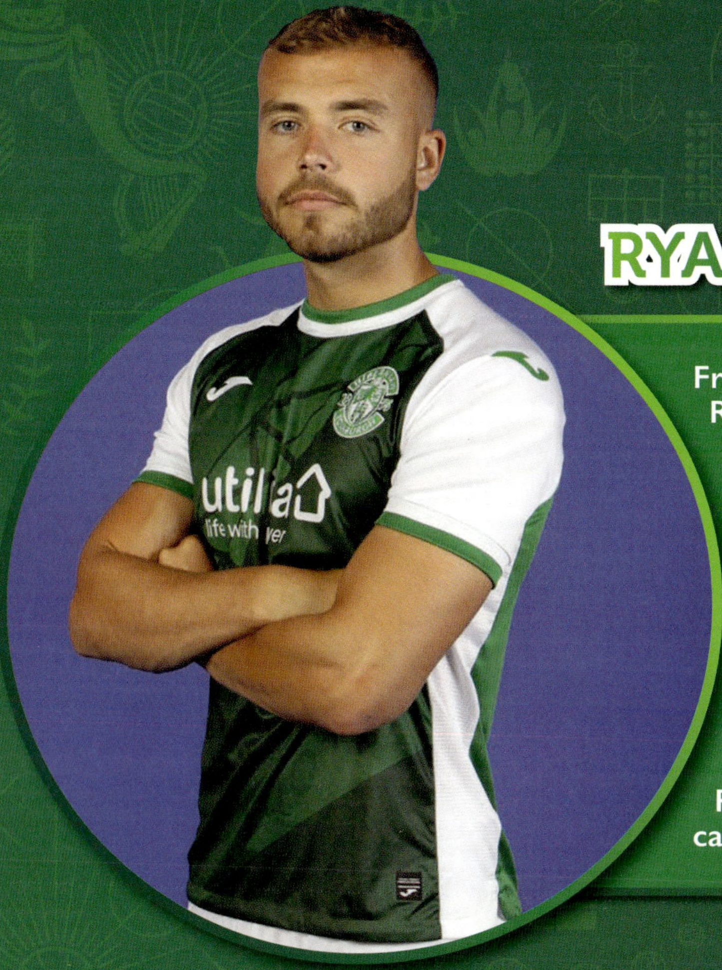

RYAN PORTEOUS

From the terraces to the first team, Ryan Porteous is another living his dream.

No longer viewed as a promising talent, he has matured into a consistent first-team performer who should be looking to gate-crash the Scotland squad on a regular basis.

Mentored by a sporting icon – and Hibs supporter – in Andy Murray, Porteous looks every inch a future captain.

CHRIS CADDEN

Deservedly named Player of the Year, Cadden is well on the way to fulfilling the potential he showed as a young player at Motherwell who earned full Scotland recognition.

Blessed with real stamina and the strength to burst by opponents on the right flank, he is improving all the time.

Whether he's at right-back, right wing-back or deployed elsewhere in midfield, Cadden is fast becoming a force to be reckoned with.

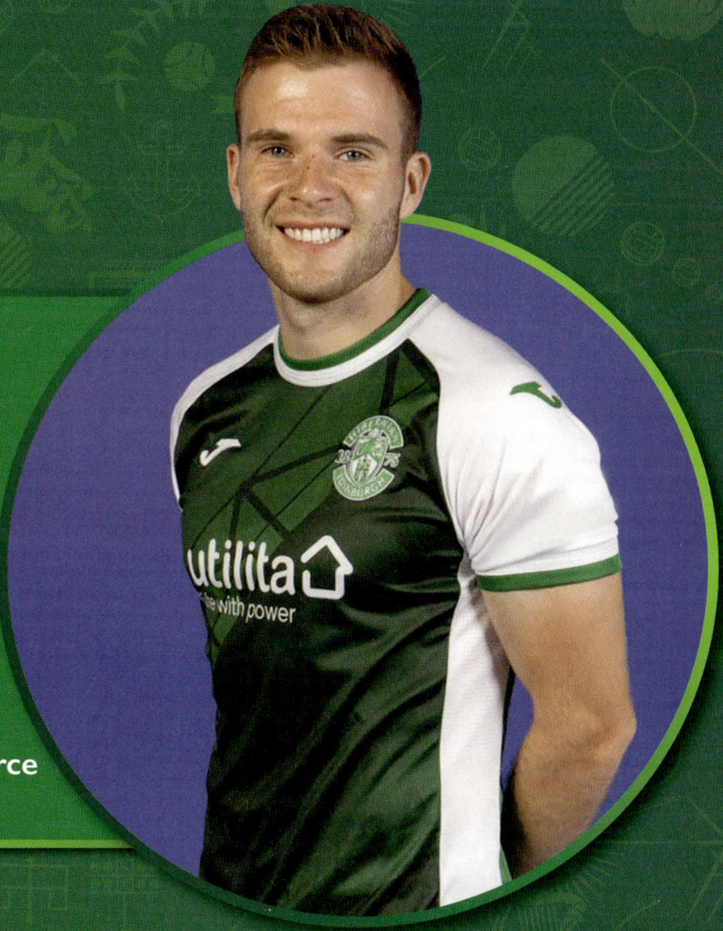

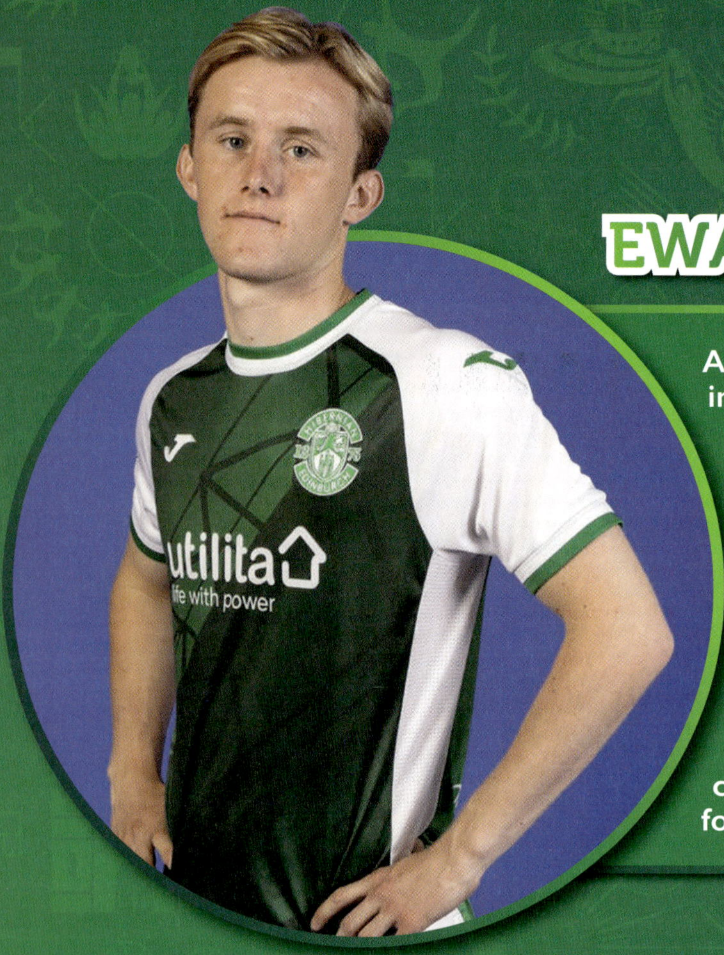

EWAN HENDERSON

An initial loan signing from Celtic in January 2022, Henderson joined permanently in the summer.

The former Scotland Under-21 international worked his way through the ranks at Celtic – tasting Premiership, Europa League and Champions League action for The Hoops.

He headed to Hibs in search of regular first-team football, and the chance to follow in brother Liam's footsteps.

JAKE DOYLE-HAYES

A Republic of Ireland Under-21 international, Doyle-Hayes can play as a holding midfielder or in a more dynamic box-to-box role.

A double against Ross County showed there is more to come from him in the final third.

Doyle-Hayes had a large group of his friends from back home in attendance that day, with supporters suggesting the club should ensure they're over on a more regular basis!

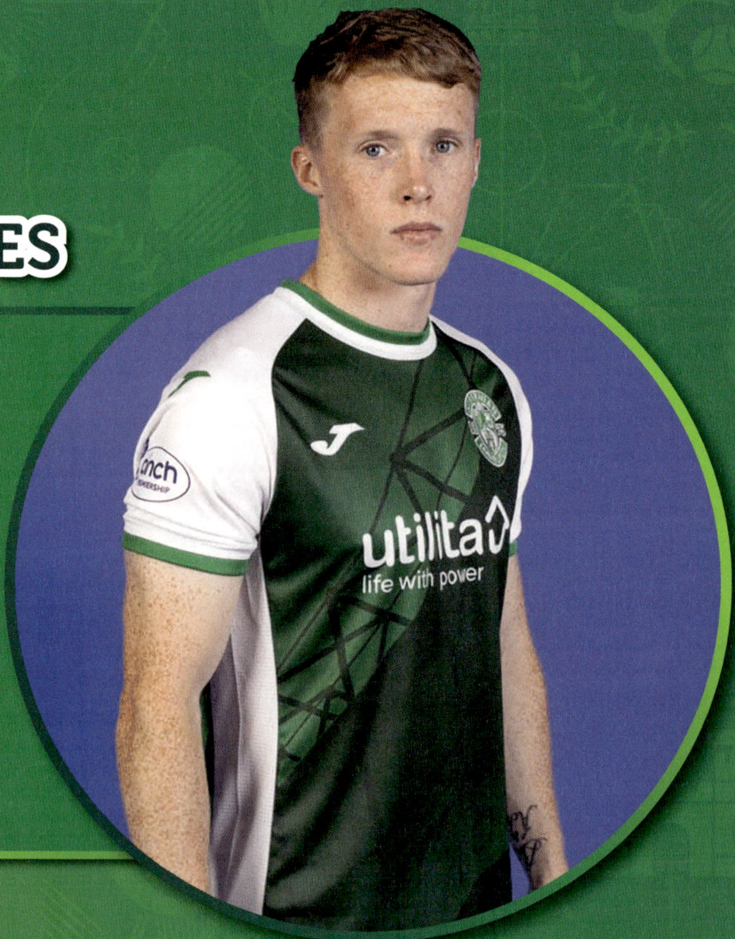

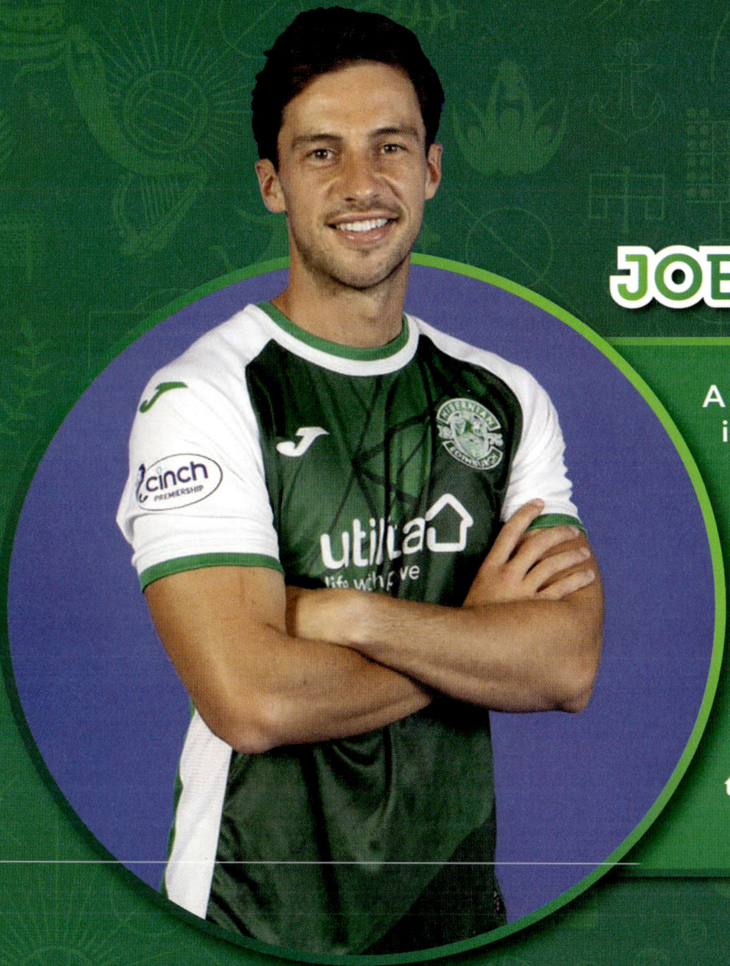

JOE NEWELL

A classy midfielder who, on his day, is capable of going toe-to-toe with anyone in the Premiership.

A laid-back personality off the pitch disguises a fierce competitor, who committed himself to an extended contract at Hibs when he had the option to return south.

It also shouldn't be overlooked that he is one of the first to offer advice to the club's younger players at HTC.

JOSH CAMPBELL

The Academy graduate and boyhood Hibs supporter had to prove himself on loan at Edinburgh City before his eventual first-team breakthrough in Leith.

A combative midfielder, Campbell endured a bit of a baptism of fire in a disappointing season by the club's own admission, but he'll be stronger for the experience.

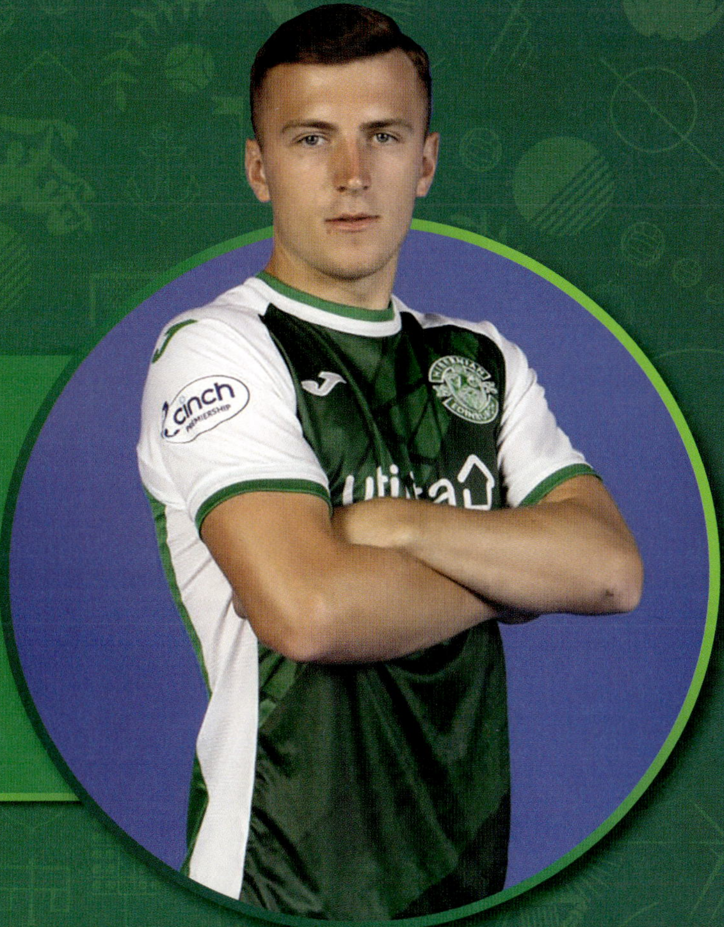

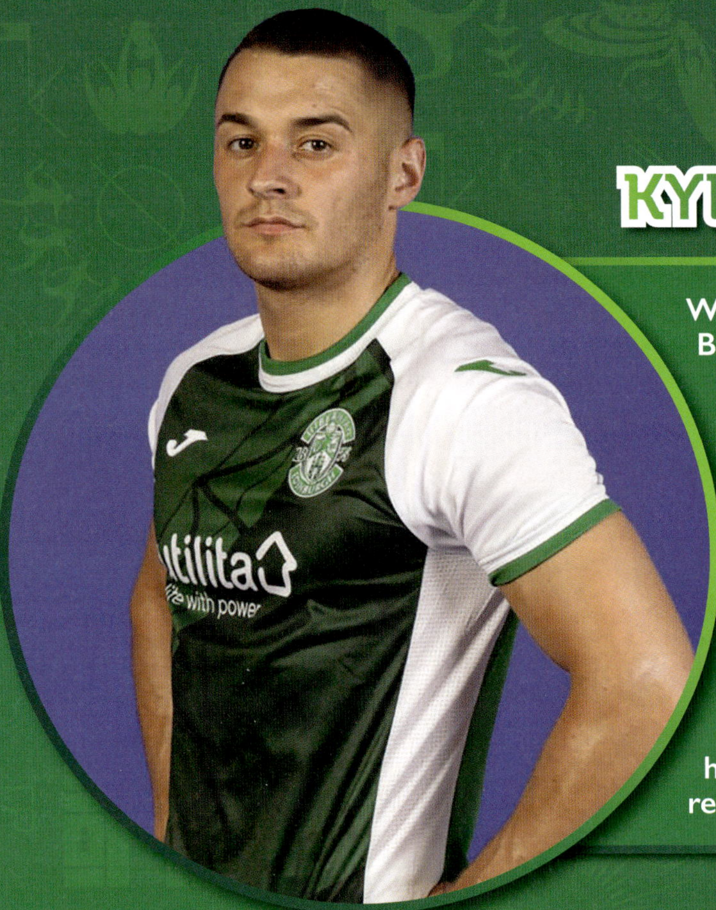

KYLE MAGENNIS

While the short-term departure of Martin Boyle left an obvious, understandable hole in the team, the prolonged absence of the injured Magennis didn't help matters either.

The former Scotland Under-21 midfielder was well on the way to demonstrating why the club worked so hard to sign him – offering physicality in the midfield and a real goal threat.

After so long on the treatment table, he deserves the right kind of break to remind everyone what he's all about.

KEVIN NISBET

Nisbet's season was unfortunately disrupted by serious injury, and the Scotland striker threw himself into his rehabilitation programme with renewed determination to return an even better player.

A good all-rounder, Nisbet is another who hasn't yet fulfilled his full potential, which is an exciting prospect for the coaching staff and supporters alike.

He will undoubtedly be a key man when he's back up and running properly.

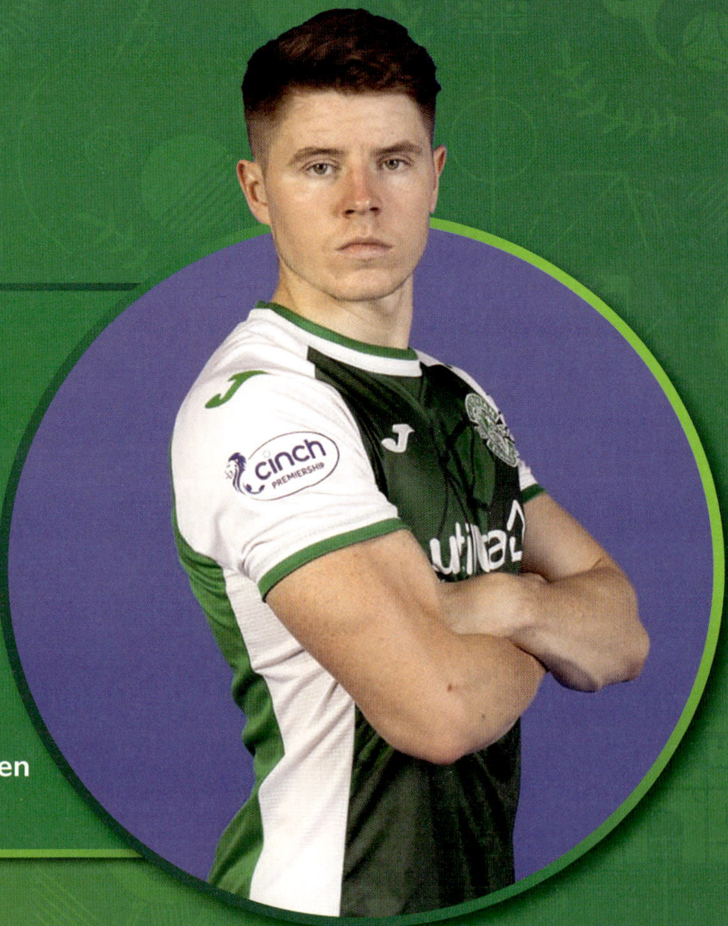

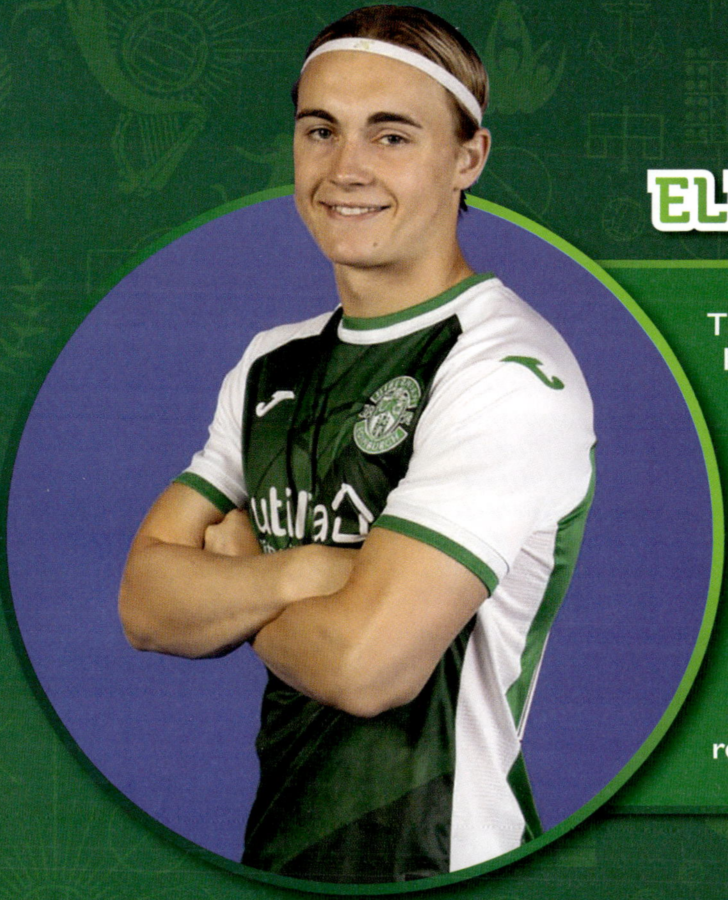

ELIAS MELKERSEN

The Norwegian Under-20 international looks to be a top talent in the making.

Thrust into the first-team ahead of schedule thanks to the injury sustained by Kevin Nisbet, Melkersen had to learn on the job quickly and a double against Motherwell in the Scottish Cup offered a glimpse of his potential.

Possessing a healthy swagger, he'll look to establish himself as a regular first pick.

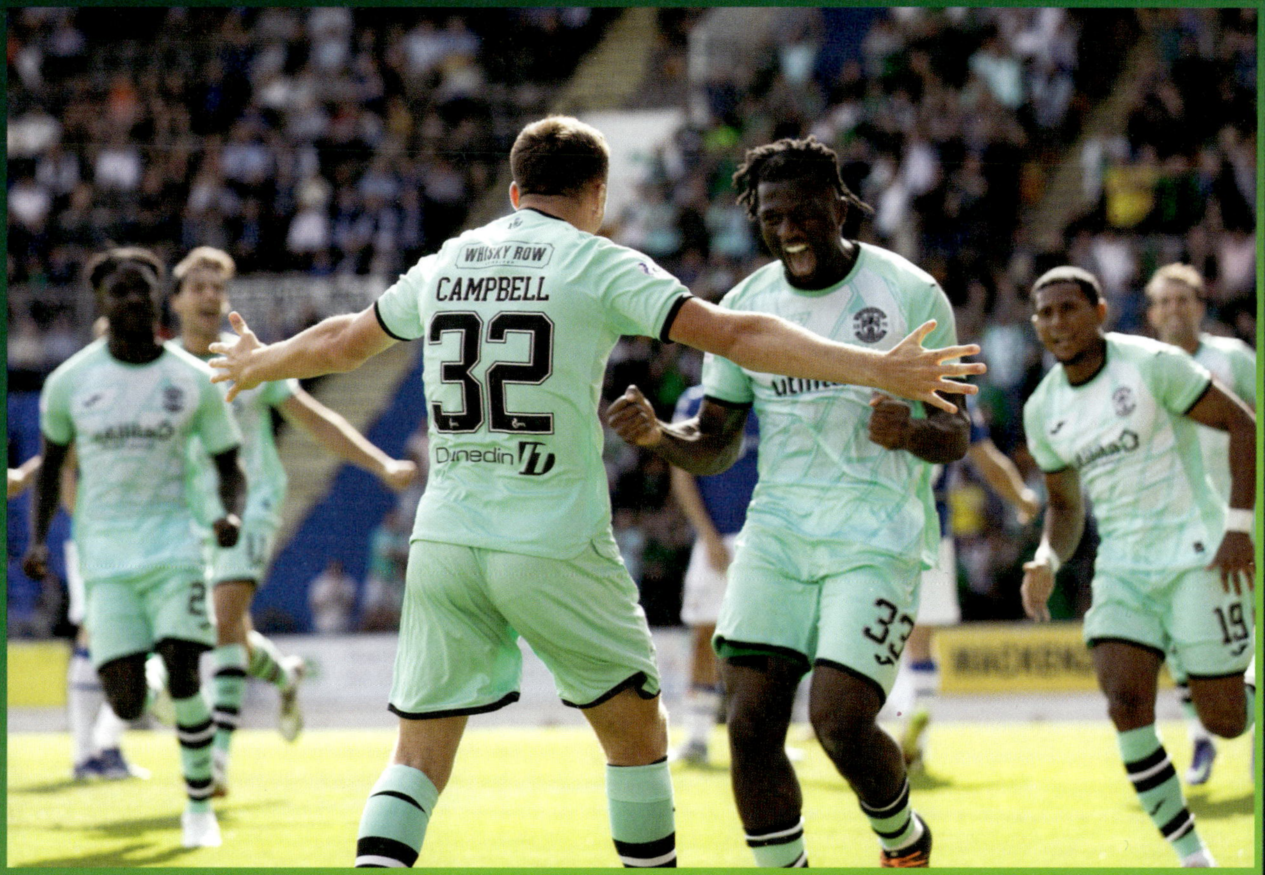

WHO AM I?

Can you figure out the three mystery Hibees?

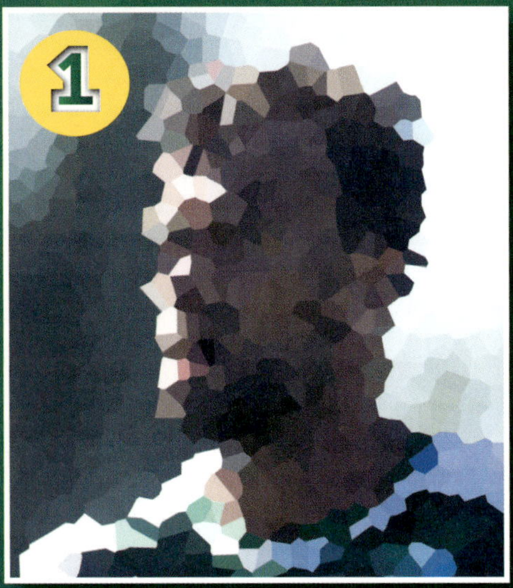

1. I represented my country at the European Championships – for basketball!
2. When I was a part-time player in my younger days, I worked as a policeman.
3. I scored my first professional hat-trick in an away game against St Johnstone.
4. I hit the target at Wembley in a Play-Off Final.
5. I kicked off my youth team career at Southampton.

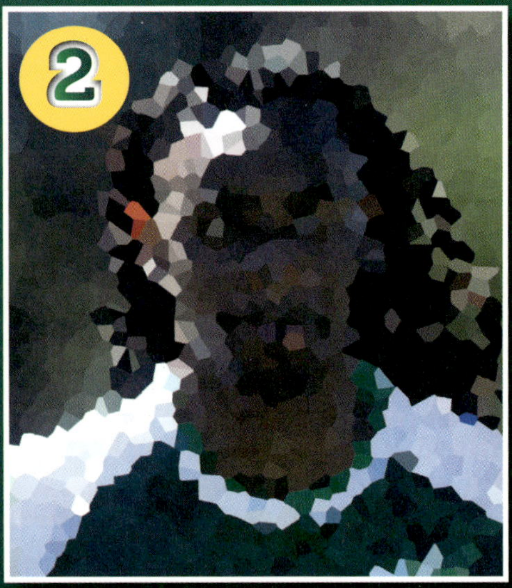

1. I was described by the club as a 'tricky winger' when I signed.
2. Celtic's Jota told me what to expect about Scottish football before I came here.
3. I have two brothers and a cousin who are professional footballers.
4. I moved to Hibs from Benfica's B team.
5. I played international football for my country up to Under-19 level.

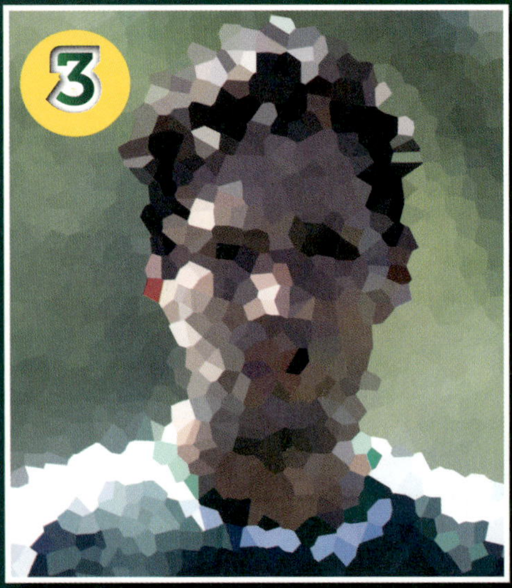

1. I initially played as a winger for Hibs before moving into the centre of the park.
2. Back in March, I signed a contract that will keep me at Easter Road until at least the summer of 2025.
3. Other than Hibs, I support Birmingham City.
4. When I'm not kicking a ball around, I love a game of golf.
5. I joined Hibs from Rotherham United.

Answers on page 58.

HIBS KIDS

SEASON 2022/23 PLANNER

St Johnstone v HIBERNIAN
Saturday, Jul 30 2022

HIBERNIAN v Heart of Midlothian
Sunday, Aug 7 2022

Livingston v HIBERNIAN
Saturday, Aug 13 2022

HIBERNIAN v Rangers
Saturday, Aug 20 2022

St Mirren v HIBERNIAN
Saturday, Aug 27 2022

HIBERNIAN v Kilmarnock
Saturday, Sep 3 2022

Dundee Utd v HIBERNIAN
Saturday, Sep 10 2022

HIBERNIAN v Aberdeen
Saturday, Sep 17 2022

Ross County v HIBERNIAN
Saturday, Oct 1 2022

HIBERNIAN v Motherwell
Saturday, Oct 8 2022

Celtic v HIBERNIAN
Saturday, Oct 15 2022

HIBERNIAN v St Johnstone
Saturday, Oct 22 2022

HIBERNIAN v St Mirren
Saturday, Oct 29 2022

Aberdeen v HIBERNIAN
Saturday, Nov 5 2022

HIBERNIAN v Ross County
Wednesday, Nov 9 2022

Kilmarnock v HIBERNIAN
Saturday, Nov 12 2022

Rangers v HIBERNIAN
Saturday, Dec 17 2022

HIBERNIAN v Livingston
Saturday, Dec 24 2022

HIBERNIAN v Celtic
Saturday, Dec 28 2022

Heart of Midlothian v HIBERNIAN
Monday, Jan 2 2023

Motherwell v HIBERNIAN
Saturday, Jan 7 2023

HIBERNIAN v Dundee Utd
Saturday, Jan 14 2023

HIBERNIAN v Aberdeen
Saturday, Jan 28 2023

Ross County v HIBERNIAN
Wednesday, Feb 1 2023

St Mirren v HIBERNIAN
Saturday, Feb 4 2023

HIBERNIAN v Kilmarnock
Saturday, Feb 18 2023

HIBERNIAN v Rangers
Saturday, Feb 25 2023

Livingston v HIBERNIAN
Saturday, Mar 4 2023

Celtic v HIBERNIAN
Saturday, Mar 18 2023

HIBERNIAN v Motherwell
Saturday, Apr 1 2023

Dundee Utd v HIBERNIAN
Saturday, Apr 8 2023

HIBERNIAN v Heart of Midlothian
Saturday, Apr 15 2023

St Johnstone v HIBERNIAN
Saturday, Apr 22 2023

POST-SPLIT MATCHES

Saturday, May 6 2023
Saturday, May 13 2023
Saturday, May 20 2023
Wednesday, May 24 2023
Saturday, May 27 2023

Fixtures subject to change.

HIBERNIAN WOMEN...

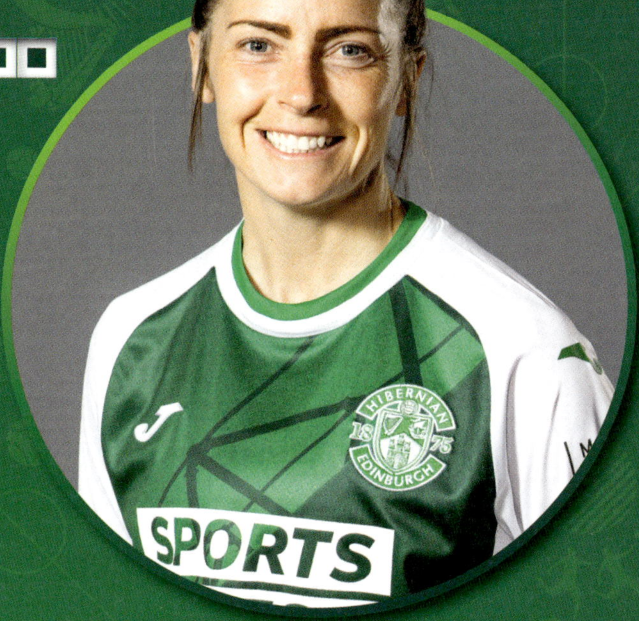

...continue to do the club proud on and off the pitch.

Manager Dean Gibson and his squad are as fiercely competitive and hungry for silverware as ever – ready to do battle with perennial powerhouses Glasgow City and the ever-improving Celtic and Rangers.

Some familiar faces departed over the summer months but a handful of potential new fan favourites arrived and it's hoped they will hit the ground running in Edinburgh.

One constant is on-field leader Joelle Murray – the club captain who sets high standards and can still barely believe she's had the chance to fulfil a childhood dream to pull on the green and white at Easter Road.

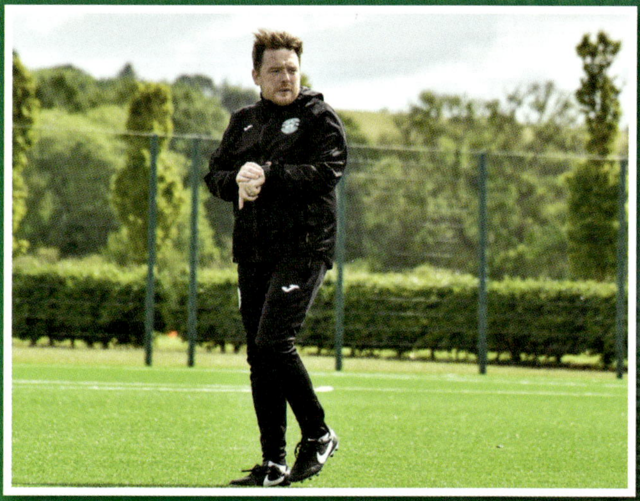

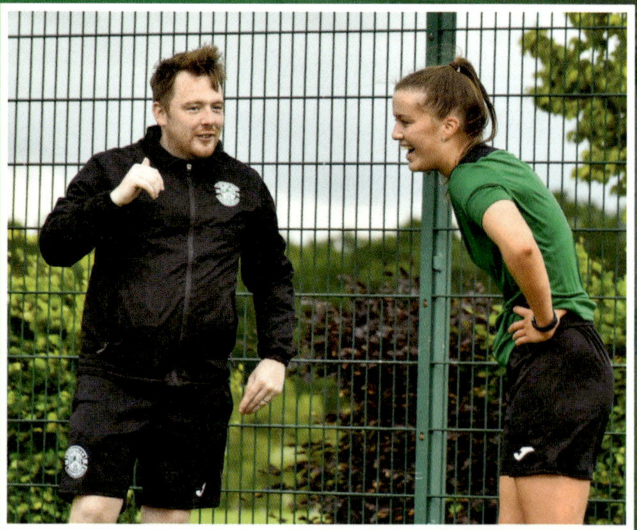

Joelle, what sticks out from the last campaign? Is it fair to say it was a transitional season?

I think 'transitional' is definitely the word. We had some real highs. On a personal note, we were proud to raise the money we did for Dnipro Kids through our alternative home strip in the colours of the Ukrainian flag. Stewart McGuire from the Hibernian Community Foundation deserves a lot of credit for that, because it was his idea. Not just the strips themselves as a gesture of solidarity but auctioning them off as well. I was lucky that someone bought mine and gifted it back to me. It shows the power of football. Football-wise, I loved being involved in the Edinburgh Derby games at Easter Road and Tynecastle. Both teams got great backing from supporters and hopefully we can carry on that momentum. It was also special to play at a stadium like Celtic Park, even if the game didn't go the way we'd hoped. We did manage to end the season well and I think that was important. We knew people were going to leave but we wanted to show what we were – and are – all about.

As a Hibee, how much did it mean to you to lead the team out in the Edinburgh Derby at Easter Road back in September 2021? Winning 3-0 probably helps, but the 5,512 spectators was obviously also a record attendance for a women's domestic game in Scotland.

Looking back on that still gives me a real sense of pride. To be the Hibs captain on the night of the first ever women's Edinburgh Derby at Easter Road, break the crowd record and get the win will take some beating. It never gets old and I never take it for granted. It's what dreams are made of. It sounds like a small thing, but seeing the West Stand full of Hibs fans and the Hearts supporters being segregated added to the competitiveness and the occasion.

A lot of hard work has been done behind the scenes to further incorporate Hibernian Women within the wider club structure. How do you reflect on that?

It's something that we want to build on, year on year. It's always going to be a gradual process and there aren't many overnight solutions but I'm really pleased with how things have developed. We've moved to a hybrid model – with mostly full-time players and some part-time players – and I always thought that was the next logical step for the team. Ben Kensell, the Hibernian chief executive, has been a driving force and he's the type of person who wants things done yesterday. Coupled with Ron Gordon's ambition, it's helped us get to this new model which can only benefit Hibernian Women.

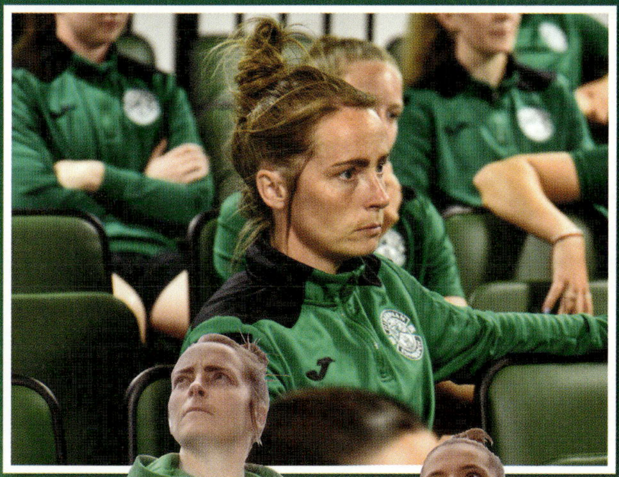

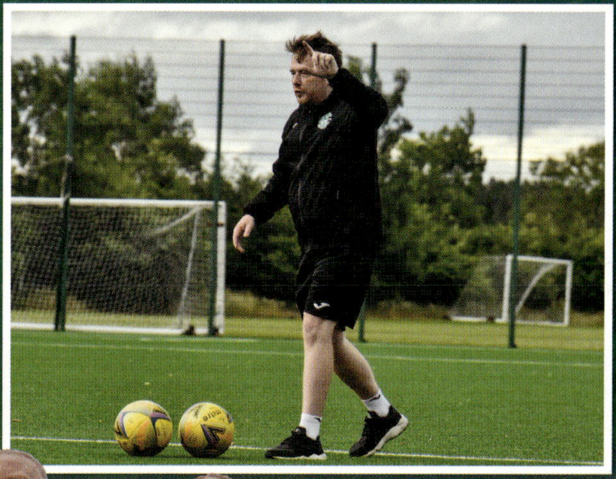

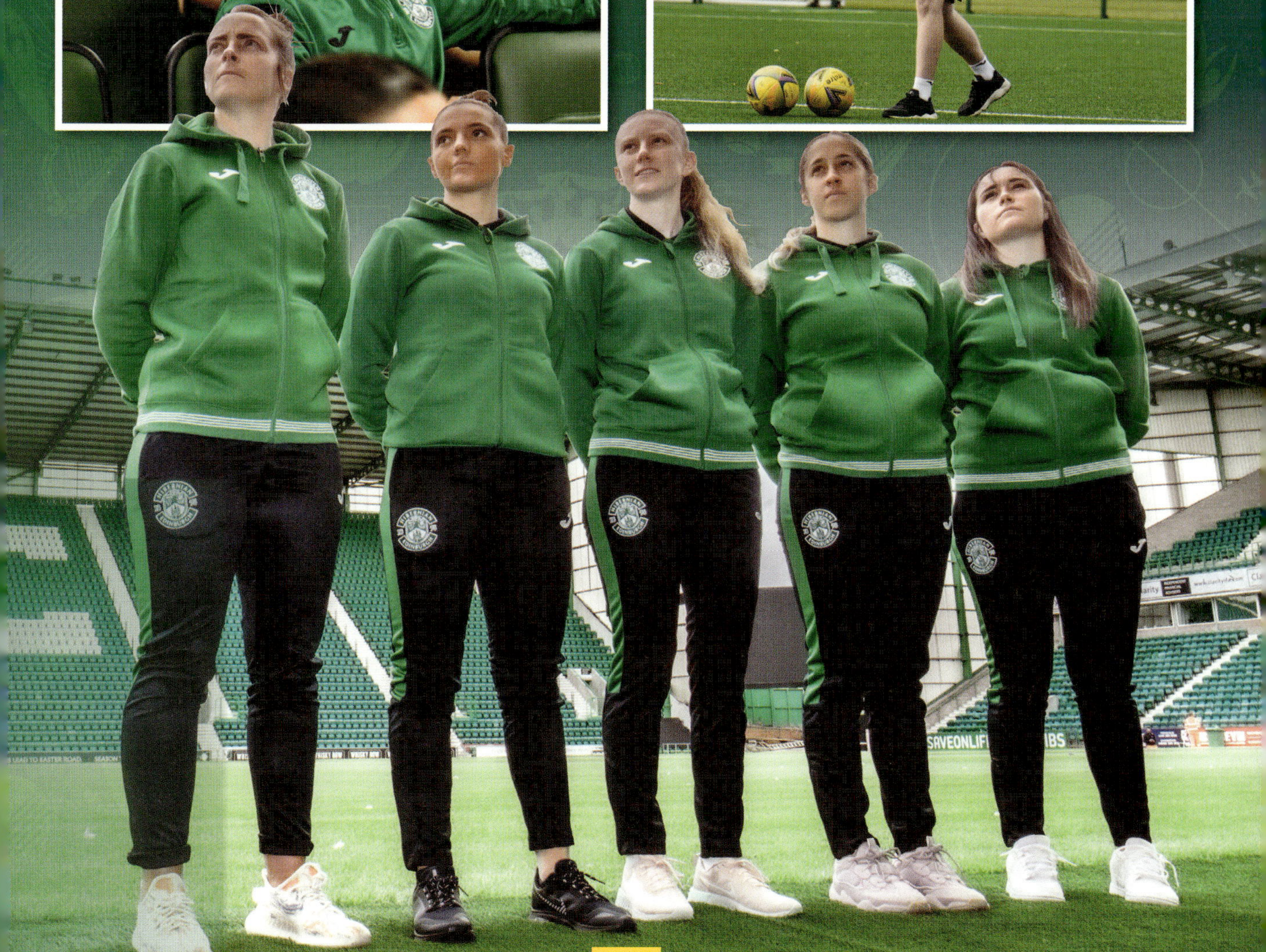

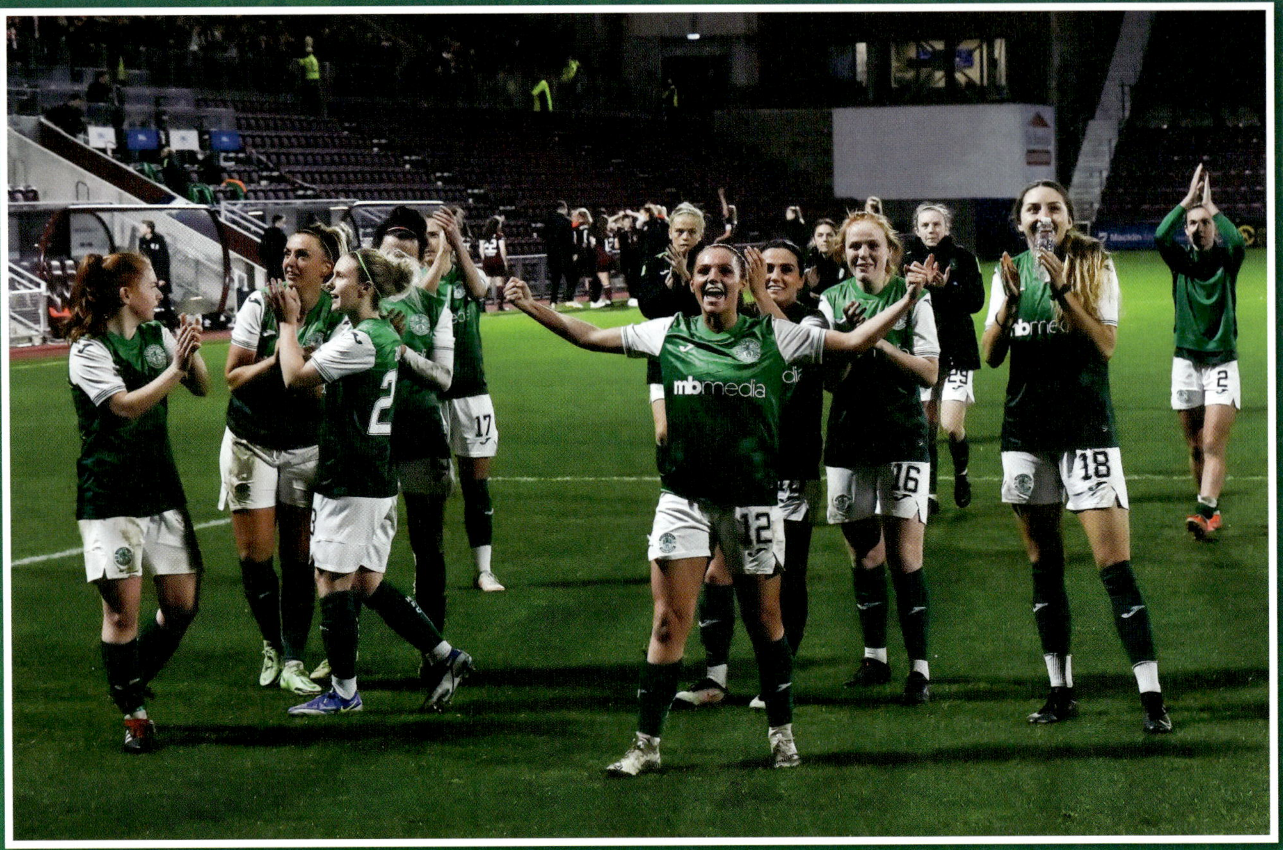

The hybrid model seems the ideal mix for those who want to turn professional and others who want to balance their football with a separate career.

I think it's important that we've been able to cater for both. Some people are in full-time education or employment and don't want to have to make a choice between one or the other. Ellis Notley, for example, was our Hibernian Women's Player of the Year last year but she's also a teacher at Ross High School. She manages to combine both areas of her life really well. We'll have teething problems and that's only natural, but there's a real desire to take things to the next level.

You've combined playing with working within the Hibernian Community Foundation but your own role's evolved. Tell us a bit more about that.

I was Girls' Academy Manager, which fell under the Community Foundation, and I felt I'd maybe taken things in that role as far as I could. I had some really good conversations with Ben and Ron, which resulted in me being integrated into the club to look at a few different things. One of those is building Hibs Kids up again to increase awareness and the membership. It's a bit of a passion project that because I was a Hibs Kid myself back in the day, along with people like Siobhan Hunter.

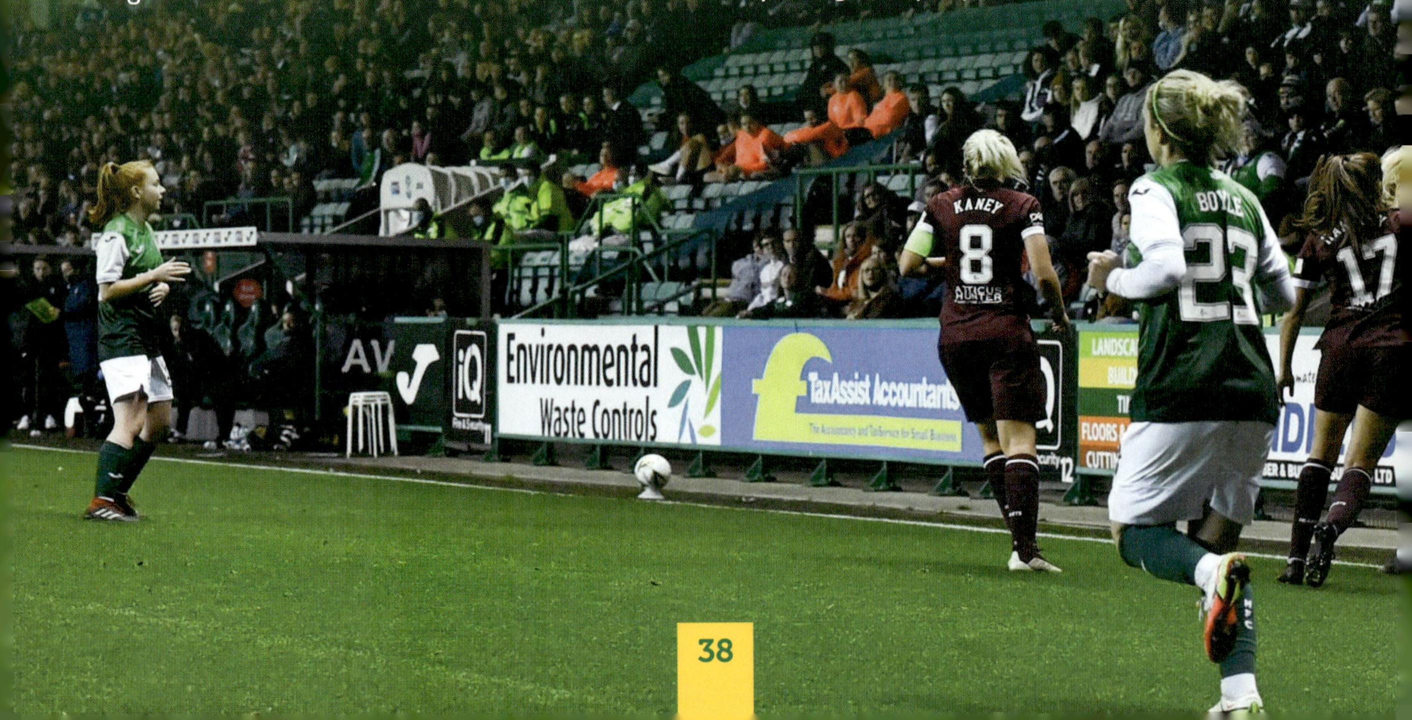

Having said all that, you're still focused on your football. What would success look like for season 2022/2023?

We've signed a good few new players, so that's always exciting. It brings a freshness to the squad, while we still have a lot of the group who are used to competing year in, year out for silverware. Last season, the biggest frustration was a lack of consistency. I don't think we put together a four or five-game winning streak. We'd get to that point and draw or lose, so we want to maintain consistency and be better in the bigger games. Against Rangers, I thought we were good and there were games when we should have taken at least a point. Similarly, against Glasgow City and Celtic we could have done better at times. So, longer winning streaks and see where it takes us. We've got new players, new staff and a new working environment so there's a lot to be excited about.

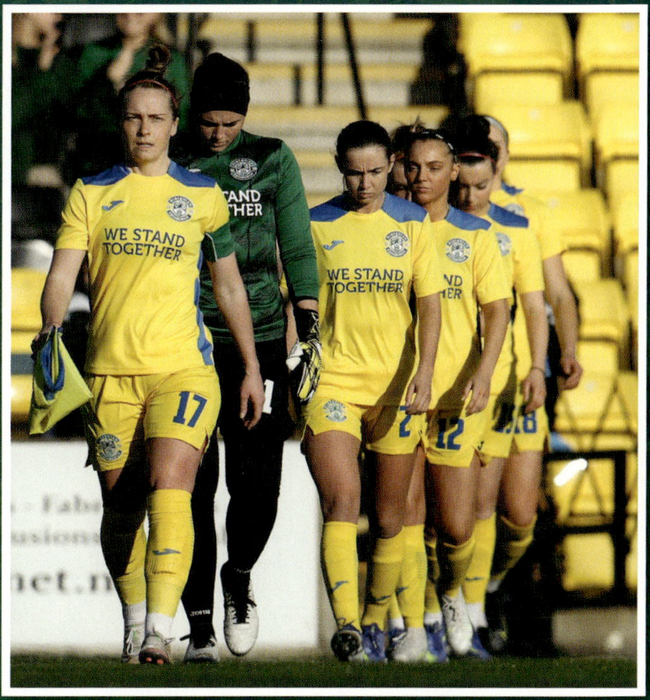

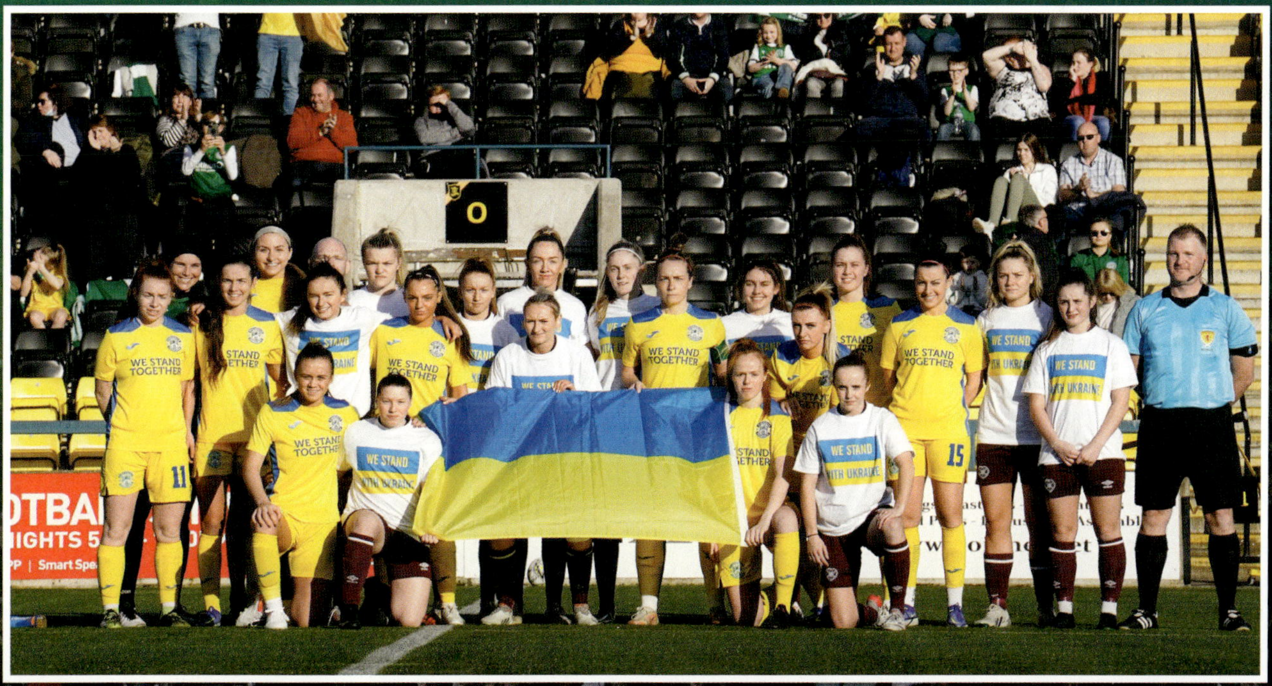

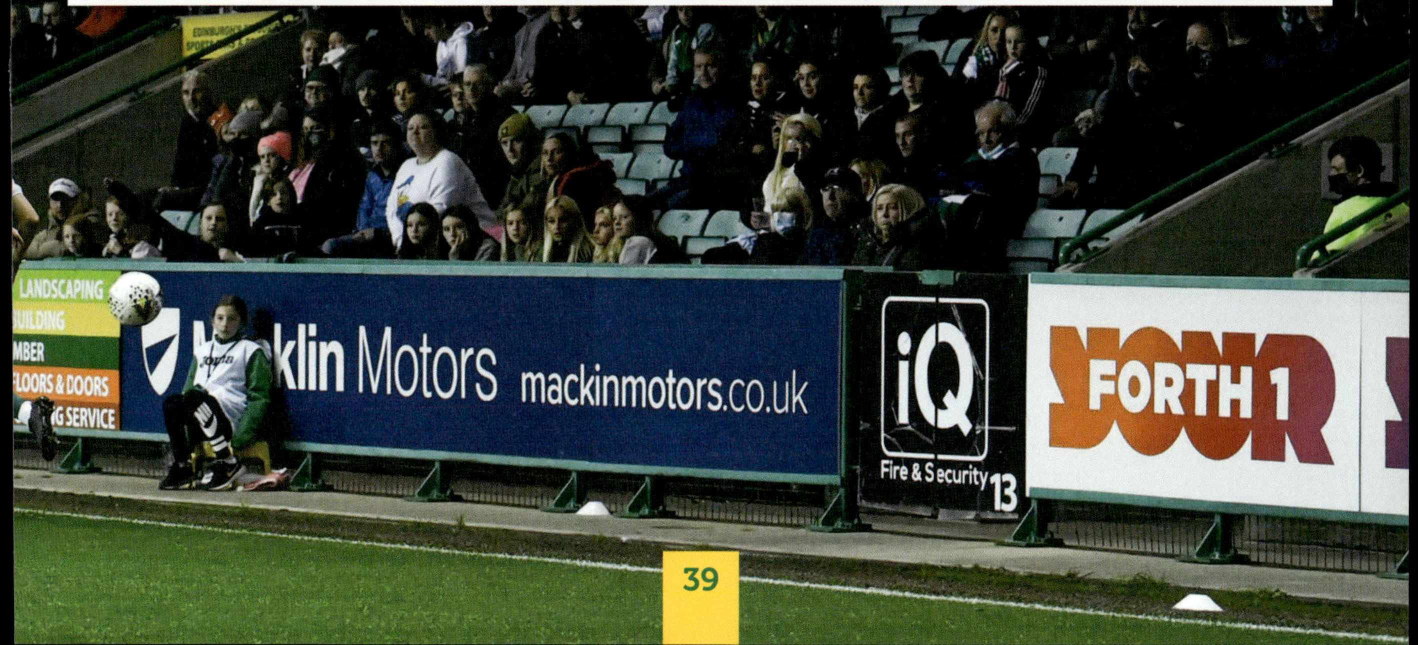

KEVIN DABROWSKI

There can't be many players who have achieved Kevin Dabrowski's level of popularity at Hibernian with so few first-team games behind them.

That says it all about the Polish goalkeeper's larger-than-life personality and his obvious dedication to both the club and his own game.

So, there was collective pride when he marked his first senior start for The Hibees with a Man of the Match display in an Edinburgh Derby against Hearts.

If the all-action performance wasn't enough, his emotional post-match interview sealed his cult hero status.

Looking back on a real landmark moment in his young career, he said: "I'd been waiting for that moment for a couple of years. There was a couple of ups and downs, and I'd been on the bench 40 times and not been used.

"The amount of times I'd been told I might play…but I never gave up and kept trying to work hard. I knew that moment would come eventually and I did my best every day to get it."

It was no overnight success story and his dream was almost derailed within a week of arriving in Edinburgh.

He recalled: "What I have been through does make me more determined. I arrived in Scotland when I was just 18 years old and on my third day I suffered an extremely bad injury. I dislocated my thumb trying to save a shot from Jamie Gullan and that was before I'd even signed for Hibs.

"I was supposed to sign for six months on loan and I'd still not signed at that point, so I wasn't sure what would happen. Would Hibs still want to sign me?

"Luckily they did and I will always be grateful to this club for having that trust in me.

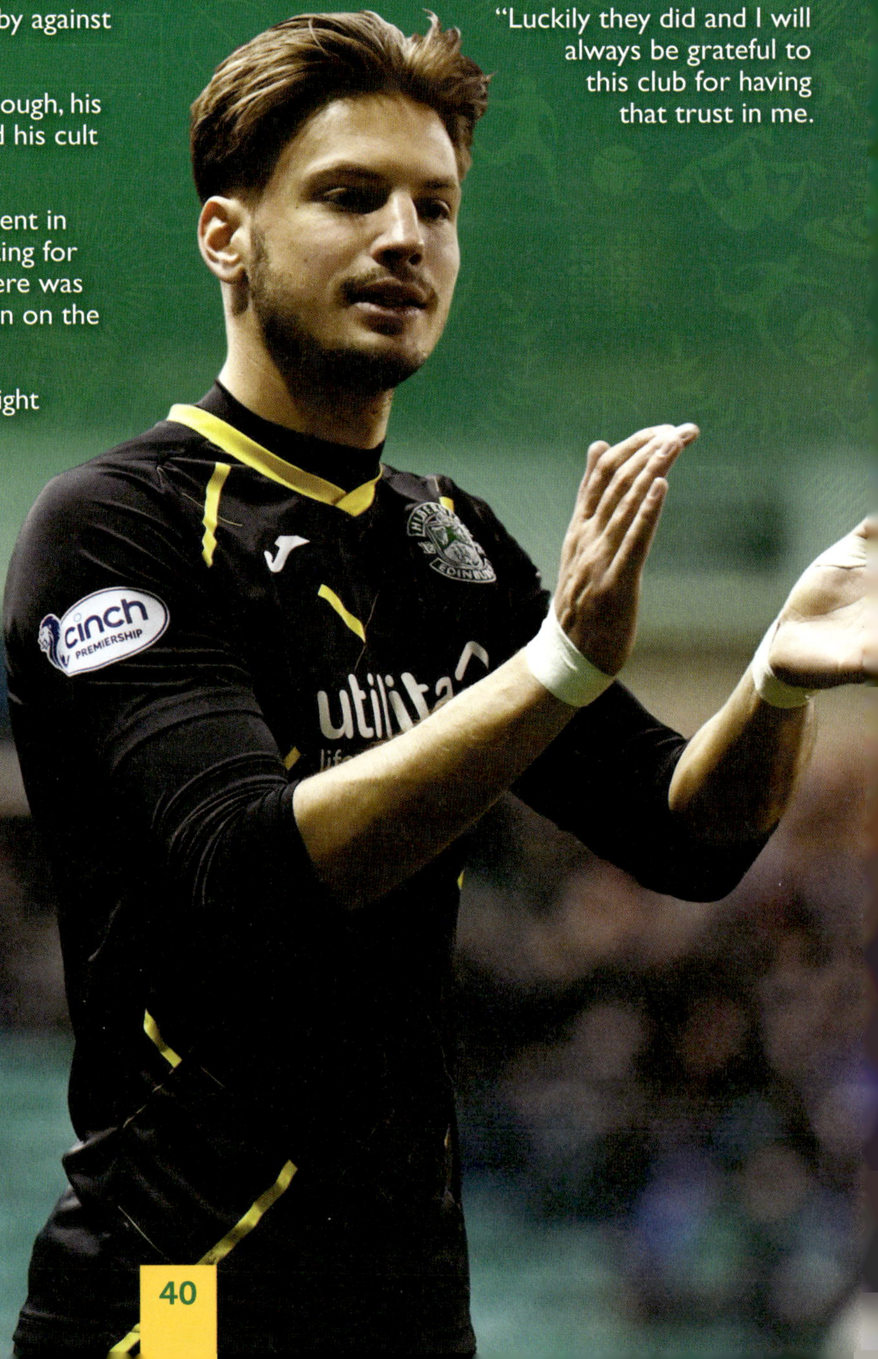

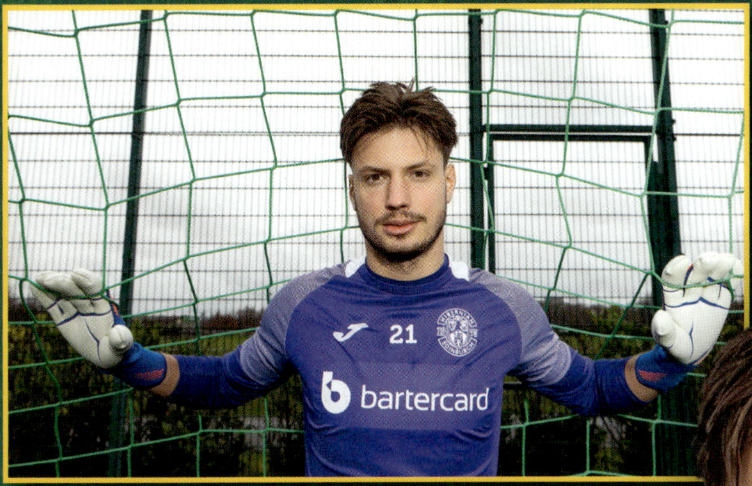

FACT FILE

Name: Maciej Dabrowski
Date of Birth: June 9, 1998
Position: Goalkeeper
Previous Club: Lech Poznan

"They took me on and let me do my rehab here, which took three and a half months. So I only had two months left to prove myself and get that contract. It was a battle but, in the end, it gave me a lot of confidence.

"I said to myself after that that anything is possible. Nothing will ever break me."

Impressive loans at Berwick Rangers, Cowdenbeath and Dumbarton followed, as Dabrowski went from strength to strength, hoping to catch the eye.

"I said to myself that I'd waited so long for my chance, so I just needed to keep doing what I was doing. I was sure I'd be able to make all the Hibees proud.

"There is always competition. I show in training that I will fight for everything – every single shot and every single ball."

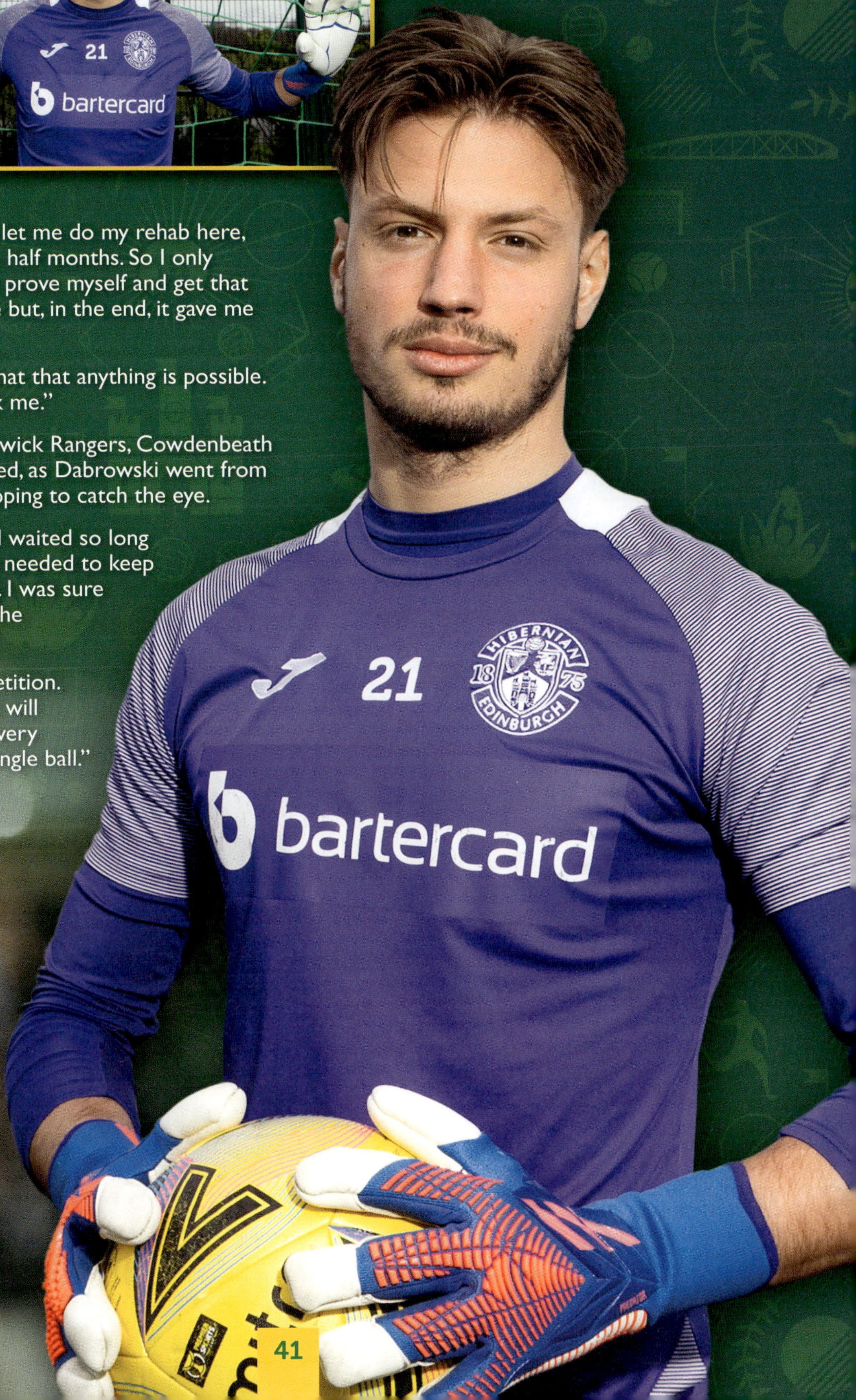

SPOT THE BALL

Can you use your judgement and skill to spot which ball is the actual one from the match?

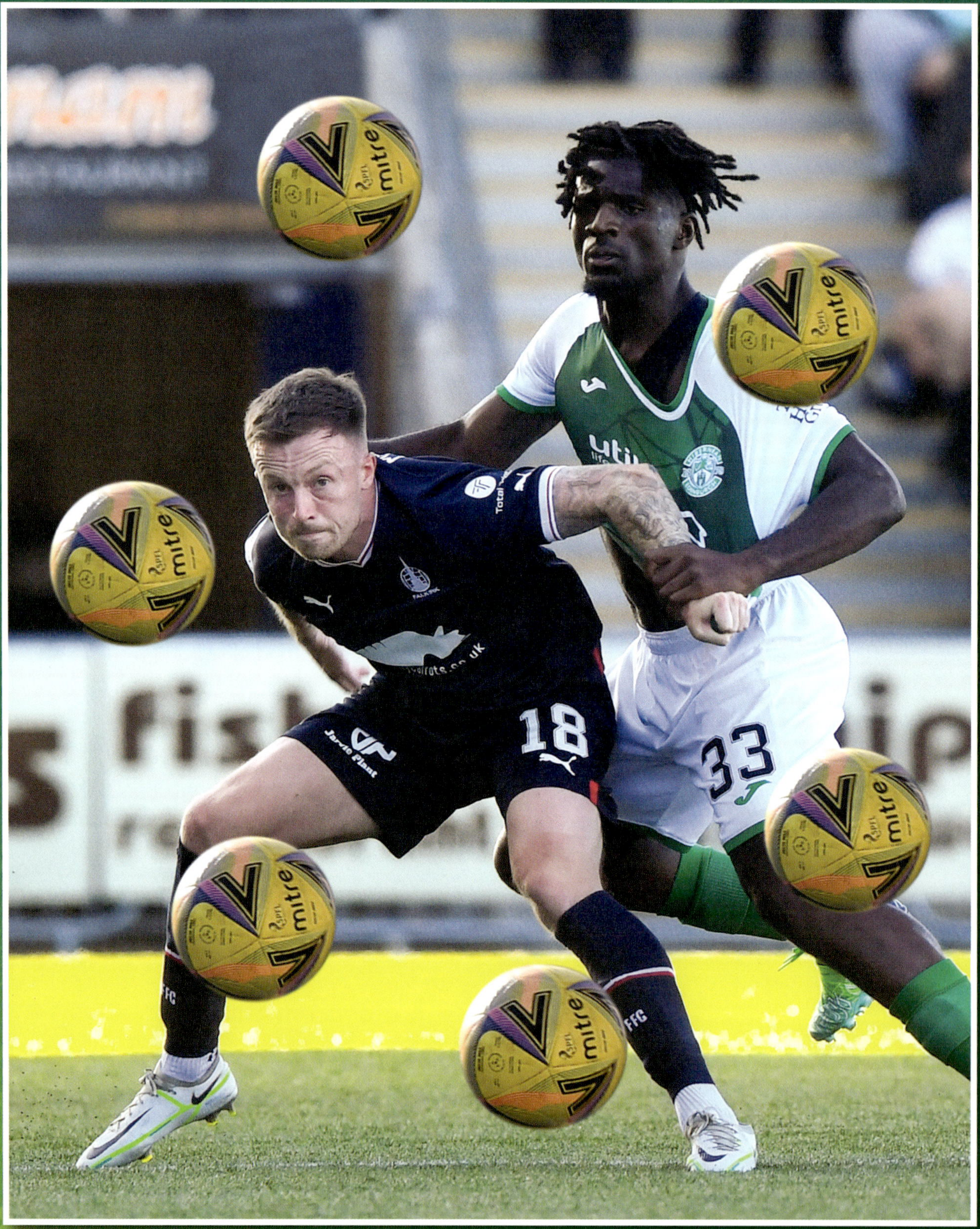

Answer on page 58.

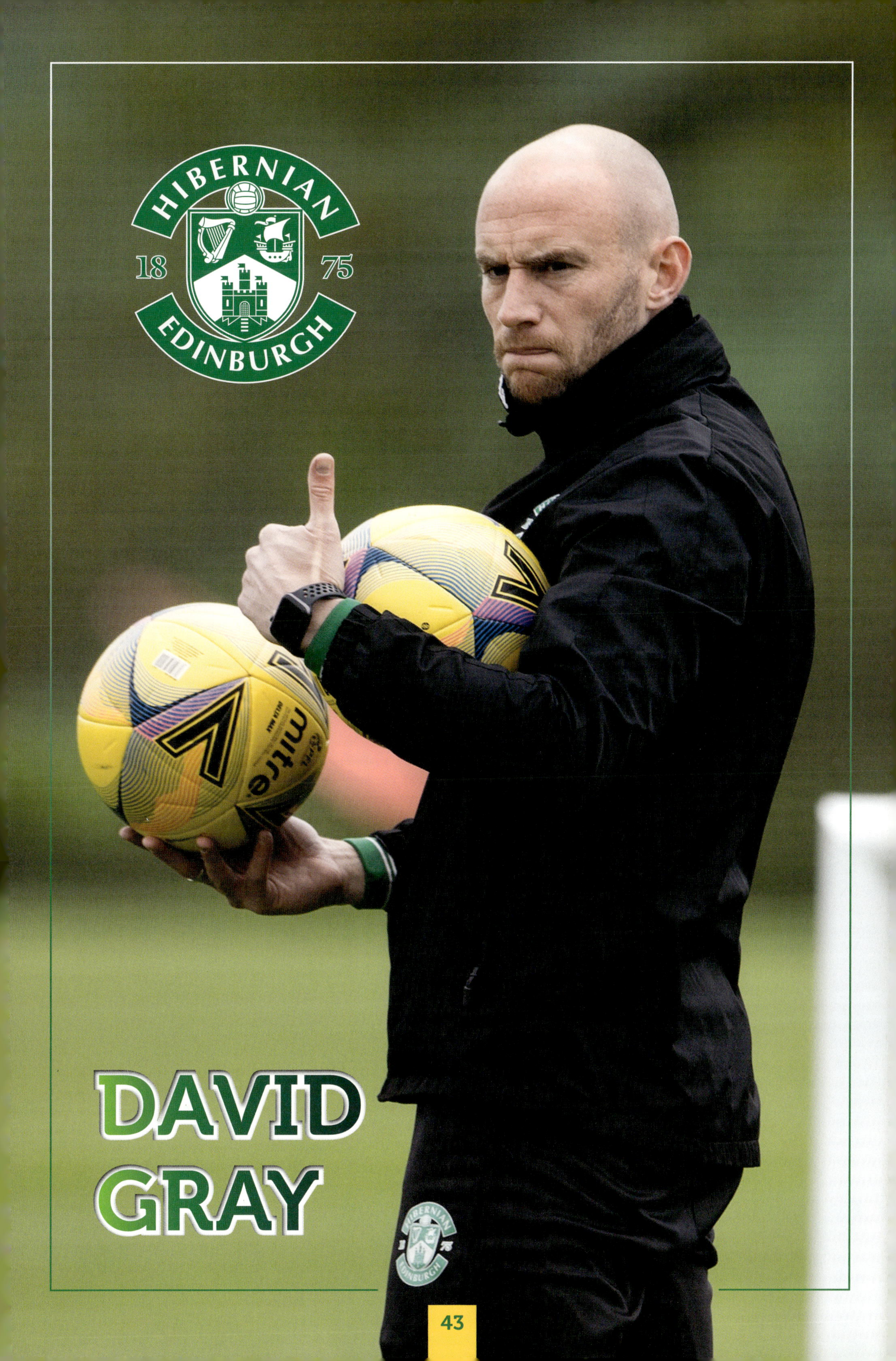

DAVID GRAY

PETER LOGAN THE KITMAN

He prefers to keep a low profile, but Hibernian kitman Peter Logan deserves to be recognised as an essential member of the backroom staff.

Since starting at Easter Road in December 2020, Logan has been a familiar face in the dugout on a matchday – with a steely determination to wear shorts, regardless of the harsh Scottish climate!

The former Kilmarnock and St Mirren man is one of the first to arrive at the Hibernian Training Centre in the morning and one of the last to leave.

He took time out of his busy schedule to explain what keeps him busy.

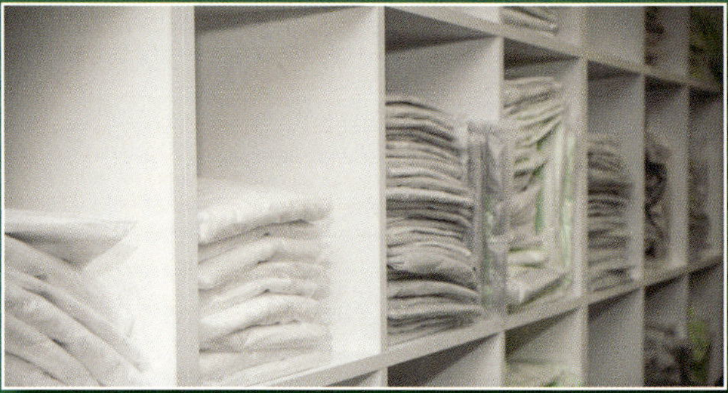

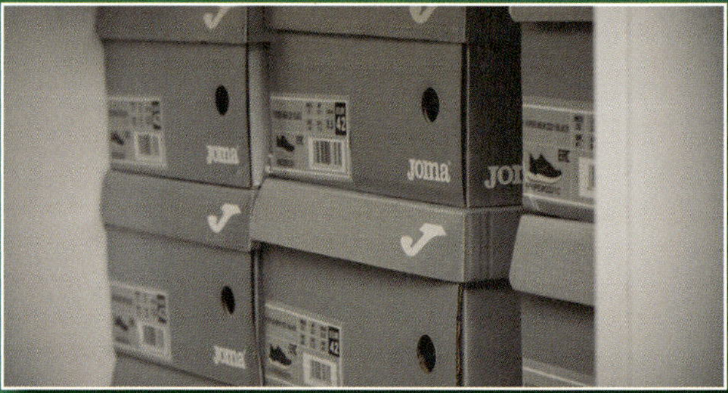

Peter, there's probably a lot more to being a kitman than most people realise. How would you describe your job?

"My job's about routine and I have to make sure everything's covered, on a matchday and for training on a daily basis. Before a game I'll pack two sets of kit for every player, boots, shin guards, flip-flops, a towel, warm-up t-shirt, jumper, trousers, rain jacket, winter jacket, baselayer tops and shorts, hat, gloves, snood… It sounds like a lot but those are just the basics and it's the same for training. That includes sorting out the Development Squad as well."

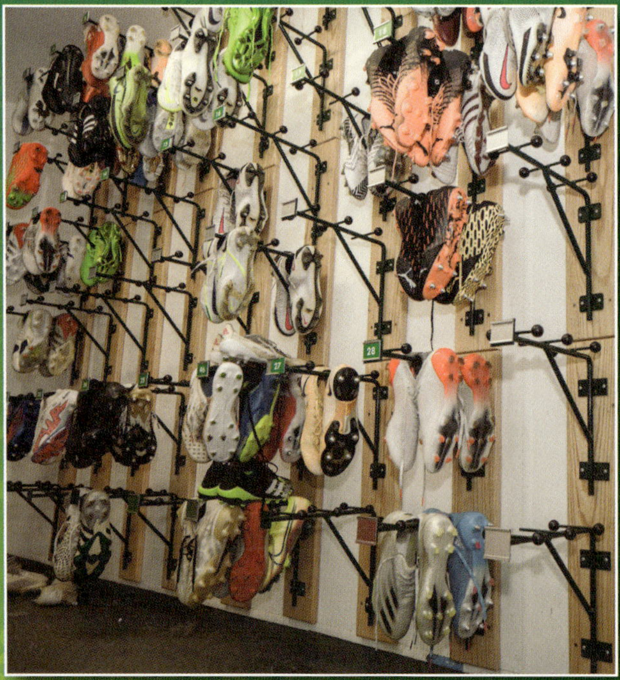

As you say, that only takes care of the basics. Every player must have their own unique quirks or requests?

"Every one of them has their own preferences. Do they want their socks cut or do they want to keep them long? Do they wear extra socks underneath for extra grip? Do they prefer base layer cycling shorts or normal underwear? You get to know the players pretty quickly and it soon becomes habit but they're all different and you have to cater for that."

What's the strangest request you've had from a player?

"I've been quite lucky throughout my career. I've never had to work with players who were particularly high-maintenance. Some of them are more superstitious than others. Craig Samson, for example, is our former goalkeeping coach and I remember he still had the same pair of shin guards that he used as a 15-year-old. The trick is just to have spares of everything so you don't get caught out. Hopefully!"

Any near-misses?

"Someone didn't put Josh Campbell's boots on the right peg before an away game at Motherwell, so they weren't packed. I discovered that when I arrived at Fir Park to set everything up. It was early enough that I had time to drive to a nearby sports shop. I was on the phone to him letting him choose. He also asked his parents to bring an old pair through with them to the game, so he was covered but it was too close for my liking."

Have you ever misspelled a player's name?

"Fortunately not. Fingers crossed I'm never in that situation because it's easily done. I think I'm so conscious of that that I'll check multiple times to play it safe. In recent times, I think Allan Delferriere's name has given me the biggest headache."

Which players are the easiest to work with and who keeps you on your toes?

"This won't come as a surprise to anyone, but guys like Lewis Stevenson and Paul Hanlon are a dream to work with. There's never any bother with them. Ewan Henderson keeps me busy. He's always chancing his arm for something."

What does an average day look like?

"I usually leave the house around 4.30am to make sure I'm at the training ground for 6am. I don't usually listen to anything on the way because I like to think through all the stuff that needs doing that day. On average I'll leave around 4pm-4.30pm. There's always something needs done."

There's a lot more to your job than just looking after the kit. Your room is always busy with people stopping for a chat.

"I think it's important the players feel like they can stop for a blether – whether it's to moan and groan or get reassurance. The rest of the staff would say the same because we're all one team here and you want to do whatever you can to support them. It just depends on the type of personality you're dealing with because everyone's different. The kit-room can become a bit of a hub and they know nothing they tell me ever leaves the room. You need to get the mood right and raise spirits when you have to. You have to be a radiator, not a drain."

You've got a special wall in your kit-room with some shirts. Talk us through those.

"I've managed to collect a few over the years. Lukas Podolski's shirt is probably my favourite because I'm an Arsenal man. When I was at Kilmarnock I'd got talking to an Arsenal scout who was there to watch one of our players. He passed on the number for their kitman and I got in touch, said I was going down for a game and wondered if he had time for me to pick his brain on a few things. He was great and he gave me two-and-a-half hours of his time, along with that shirt. I've got a few international shirts as well from some of the boys in here, like Scotland ones for Kevin Nisbet, Ryan Porteous, Paul McGinn or overseas ones from guys like Alex Gogic, Martin Boyle and Ofir Marciano. There's still space for a Thierry Henry Arsenal one if he happens to read this..."

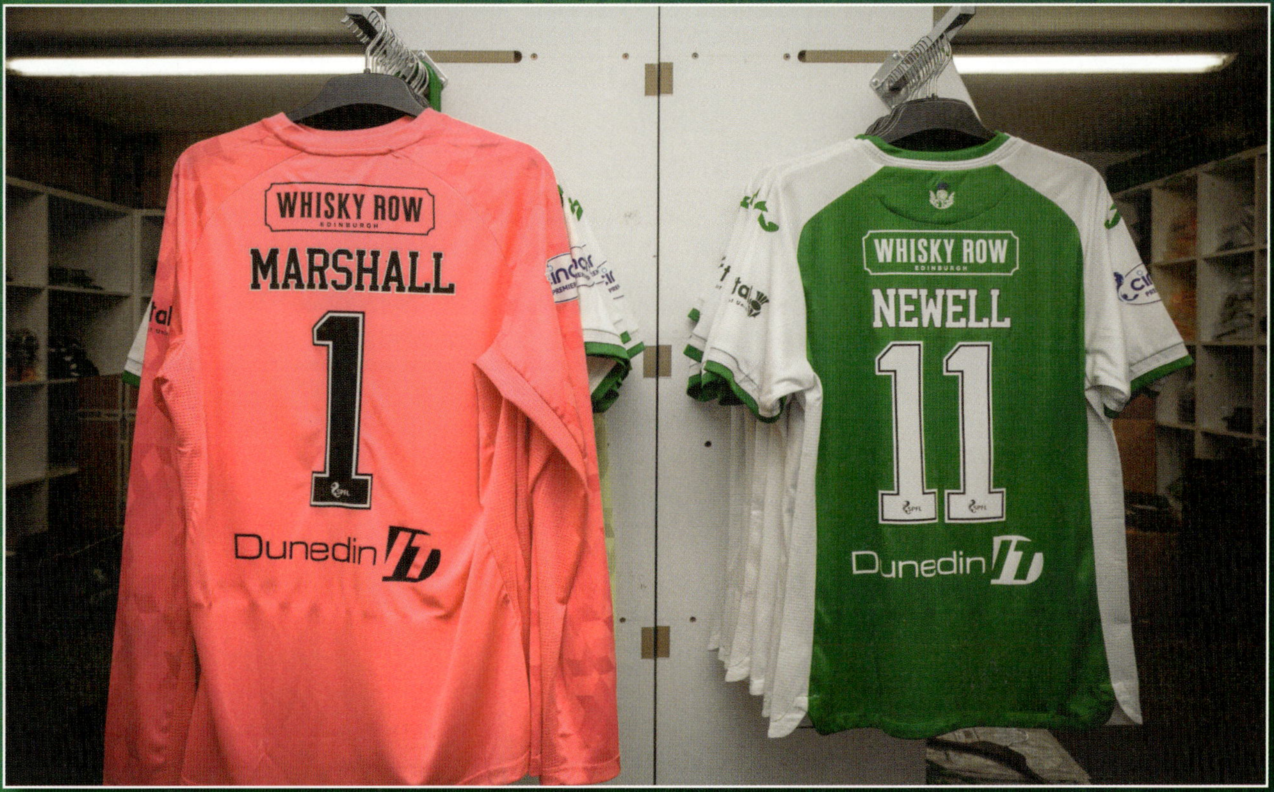

PLAYER CHAT

We took a look behind the scenes at HTC and enlisted the help of a secret footballer to spill some secrets about life at Hibernian. Can you guess who's who?

1 The dark horse in the gym. No matter how many miles are on the clock. He's a machine.

A
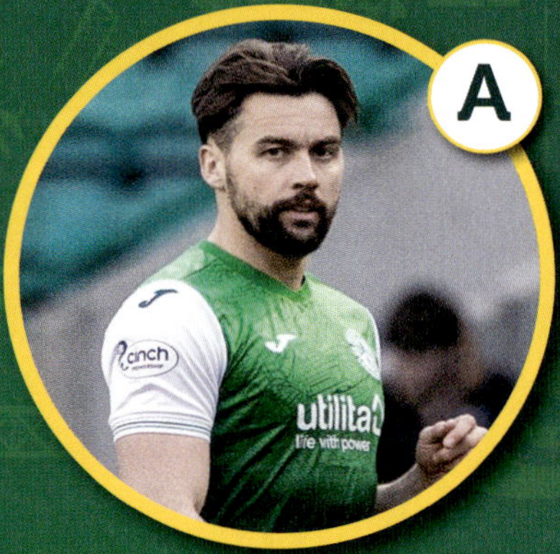

B
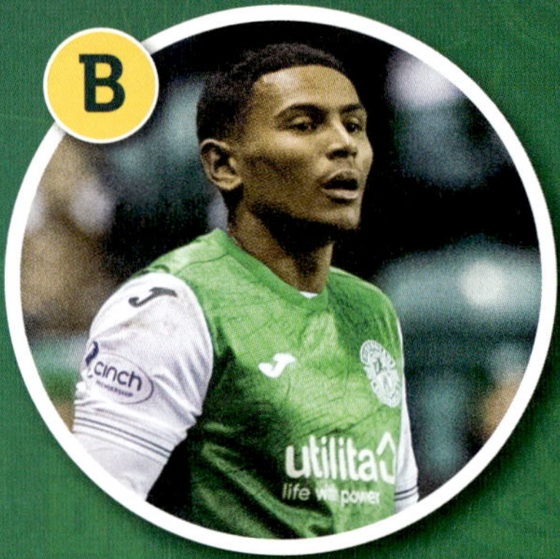

2 We all respect him, but he does love a quote from Ted Lasso. He's recommended it to a few of us.

3 The big man spends the longest on his hair – at least since Scott Allan left – but, to be fair, it looks magnificent.

C
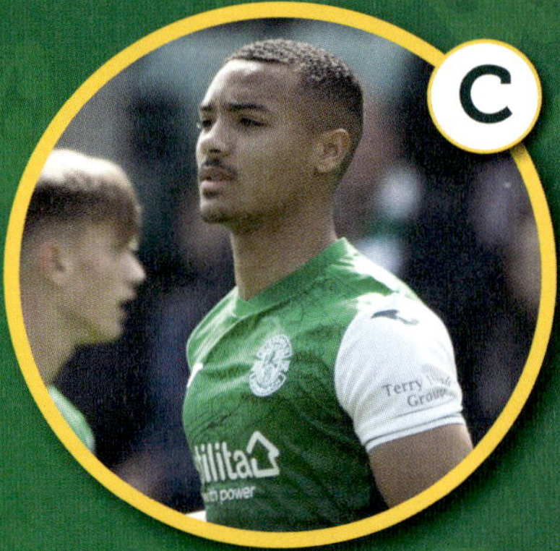

D
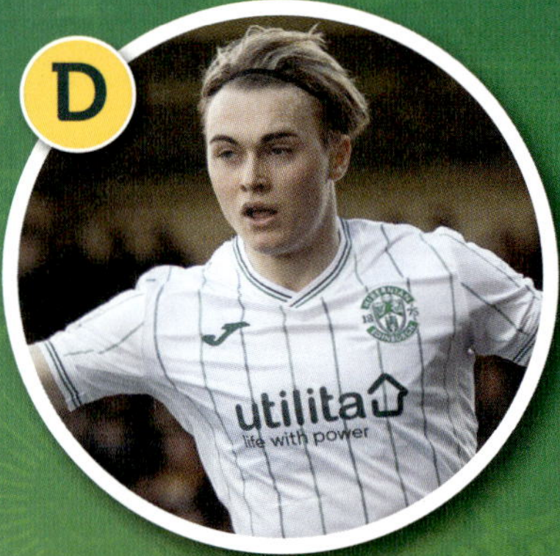

4 He takes his fashion as seriously as his football. He doesn't care what the boys think of his clothes.

5 His signing video on the club twitter made us laugh, but we don't think he'll be winning any acting awards.

E
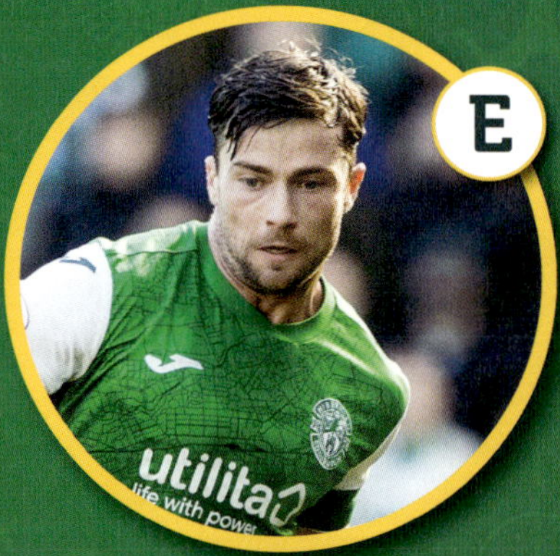

6

He'll be the first to moan if something goes wrong in a game or training, but only because he has really high standards.

F

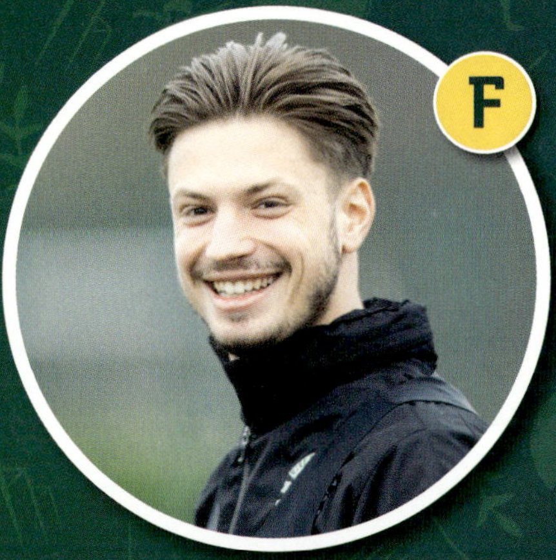

G

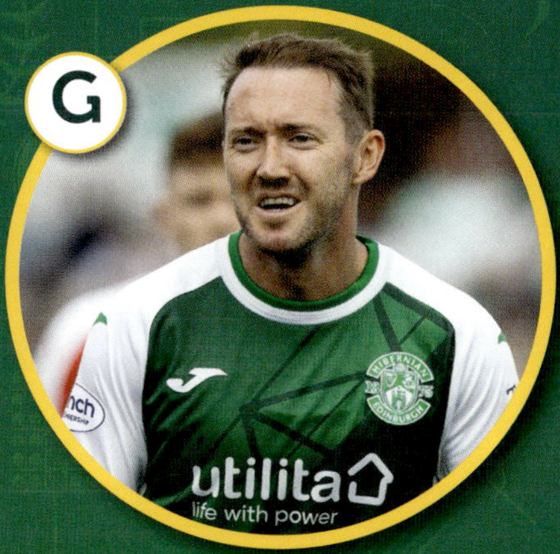

7

When he retires they should build a statue of him. Even just his hands.

8

I have never seen this man without a smile since he signed for the development squad and joined in with the first team. He's the same on social media.

H

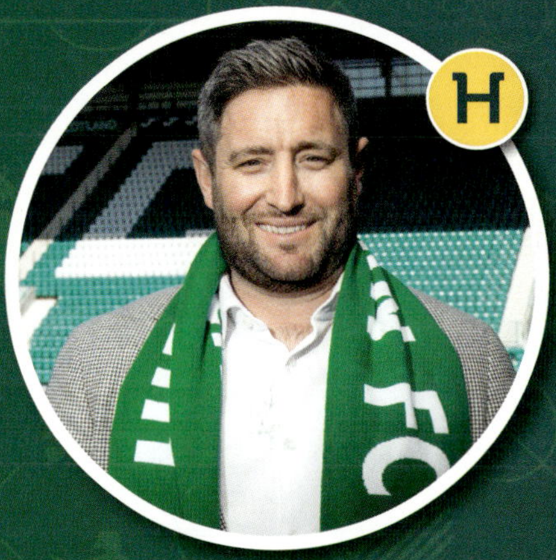

I

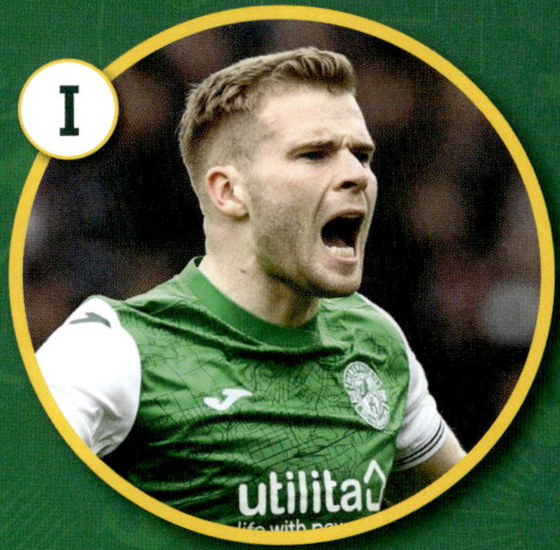

9

If you've had a bad day, you want a hug from this guy. No arguments.

10

He's like the Duracell bunny. You're not keeping up with him on long runs or sprints.

J

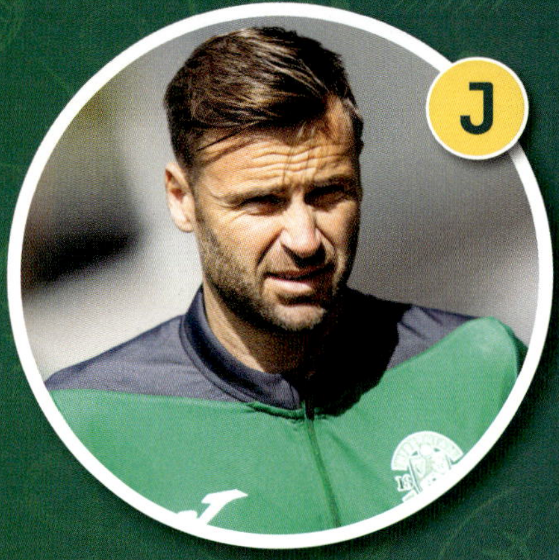

Answers on page 58.

LOCAL HERO: PAUL HANLON

Paul Hanlon is the boyhood Hibee who has lived his dream.

The kid from the terraces is now club captain, with more than 500 appearances under his belt.

Immortalised in song, in possession of a Scottish Cup winners' medal and responsible for some fine charitable deeds in the community through the foundation he set up with long-time friend and team-mate Lewis Stevenson, he is every inch the modern-day club legend.

On the landmark appearance, he spoke for anyone who has ever dreamed of pulling on the green and white.

He said: "To reach this milestone at Hibs is something I'm really proud of. It was a dream for me to play once for this club, so to do it 500 times is great and hopefully I've got a few more in me."

David Gray – another long-term friend and now coach – added: "At any level, it's great to play 500 games but to do it at one club…

"Paul knows exactly what it takes to be successful at Hibs, through tough times and in good times. He's an example for everyone at the club."

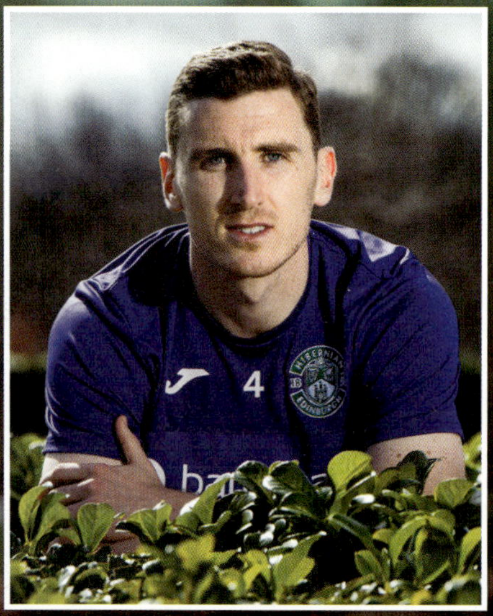

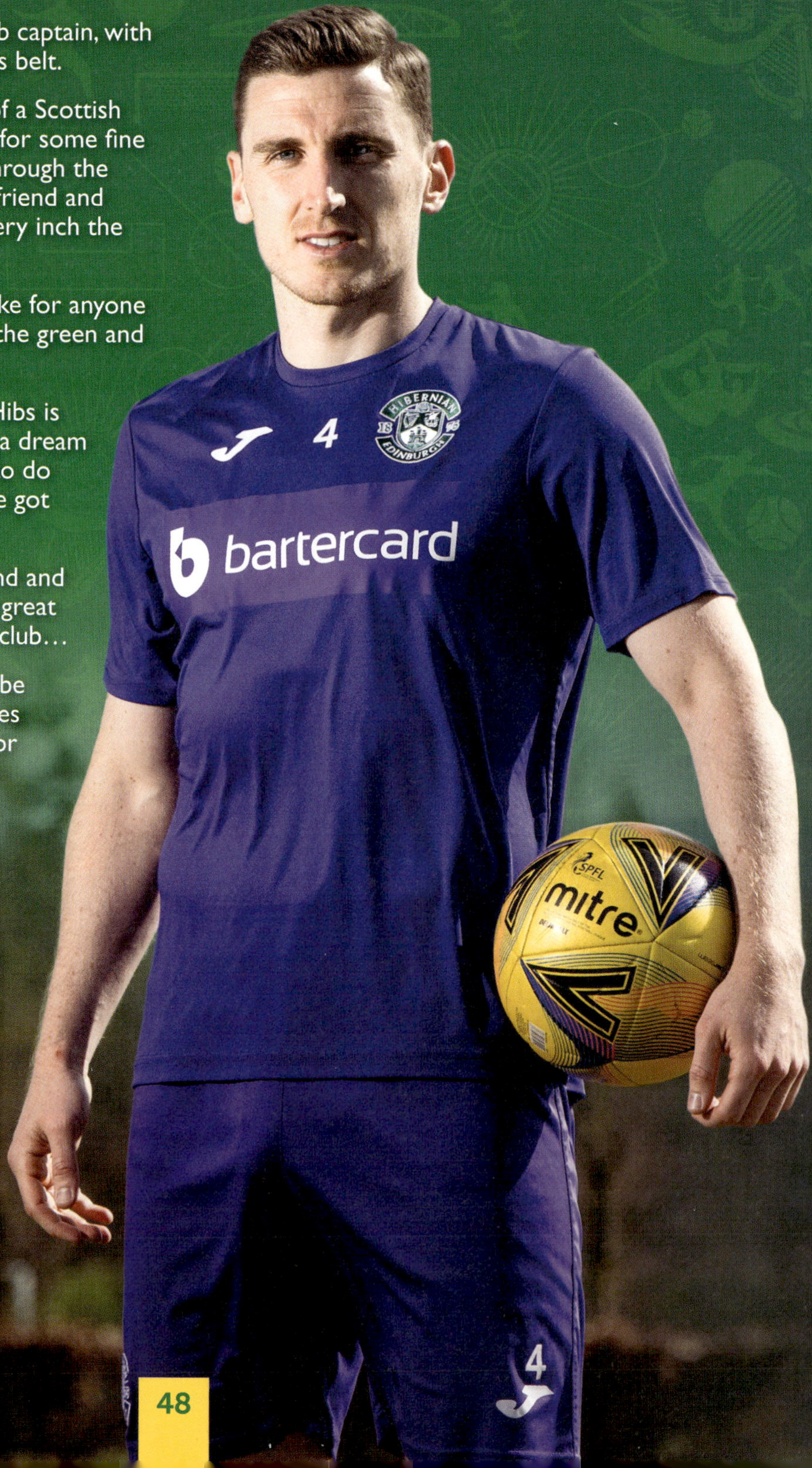

FACT FILE

- Paul grew up as a Hibernian season ticket holder, and his favourite player was Franck Sauzée.
- He played youth football in Edinburgh for the famous youth football club Hutchison Vale, where he was an attacking midfielder!
- He made his first senior appearance for Hibs on January 12, 2008, against Inverness Caledonian Thistle in the Scottish Cup.
- In December 2008, he was loaned out to St Johnstone for regular first-team experience and Saints remain the only other senior club he's played for.
- In the 2015-16 season, Paul scored a memorable injury-time equaliser against Hearts in the Scottish Cup. Hibs won the replay and went on to win the competition.
- He was awarded a testimonial by Hibs in March 2018 – playing Blackburn Rovers – after which the Hanlon Stevenson Foundation was set up, alongside Lewis Stevenson.
- The former Scotland Under-21 captain was first called up to the senior Scotland squad in November 2017, for a friendly against the Netherlands, but made his full debut in a 1-0 win against the Czech Republic in October 2020.
- Paul has twice been voted the club's Player of the Year and is regarded as a real leader by his team-mates.

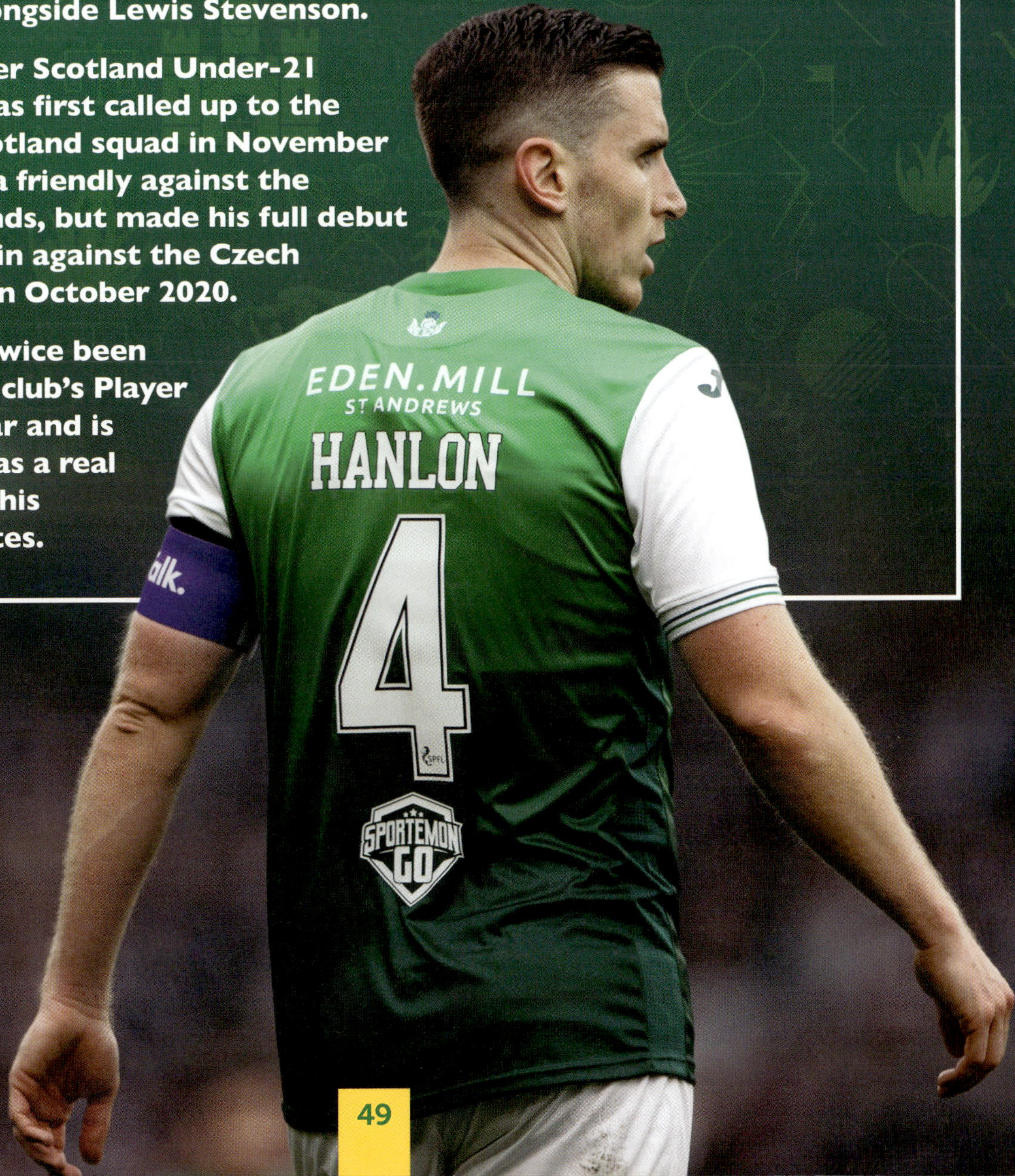

10 FACTS ABOUT... LEWIS STEVENSON

1. Lewis Stevenson was born in Kirkcaldy in January 1988.
2. Lewis joined the Hibernian Academy system at the age of 14, having previously trained with St Johnstone.
3. While he was with St Johnstone, Lewis was spotted by then-Hibs scout Mike Meechan, who noted that he 'looked a class act, even in the warm-up'.
4. He made his competitive debut against Ayr United in the League Cup, a 2-1 win for The Hibees back in September 2005.
5. Playing in the centre of midfield, Lewis was named Man of the Match in the 2007 League Cup Final triumph over Kilmarnock.
6. After success in the Scottish Cup in 2016, Lewis is the only player to have won both domestic cup competitions in the green and white of Hibernian.
7. Lewis was awarded a testimonial for his service to Hibs in 2017, when the club took on Sunderland.
8. In the aftermath, alongside close friend and team-mate Paul Hanlon, he set up the Hanlon Stevenson Foundation – which raises money to help local causes in Edinburgh.
9. Lewis has one senior cap for Scotland, picked up in a friendly against Peru back in May 2018.
10. His first nickname at Hibs was 'Bebo', because team-mates thought he spent so much time on the old social media platform.

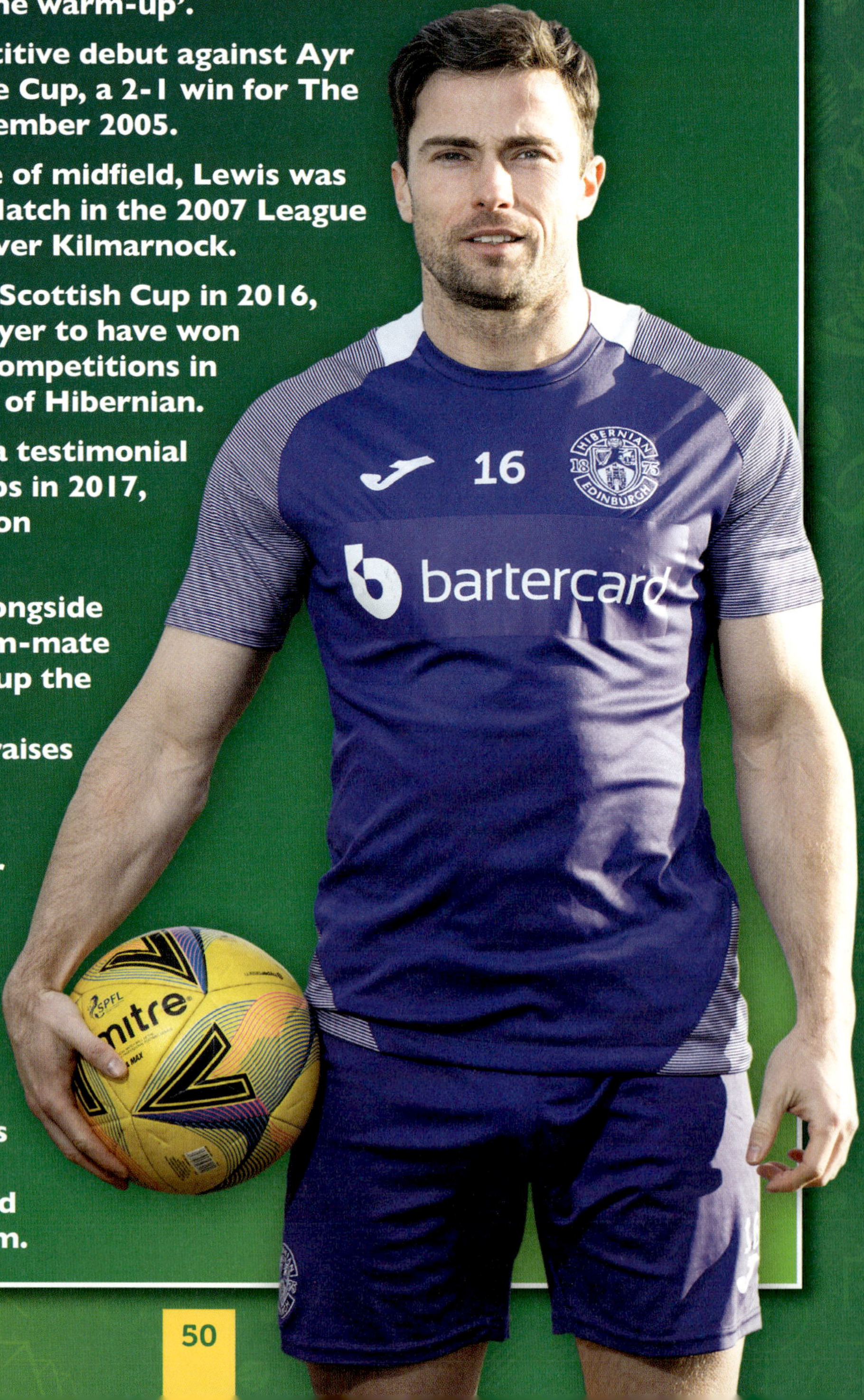

SPOT THE DIFFERENCE

Use your observational skills to seek out and spot the 8 differences between the two pictures below.

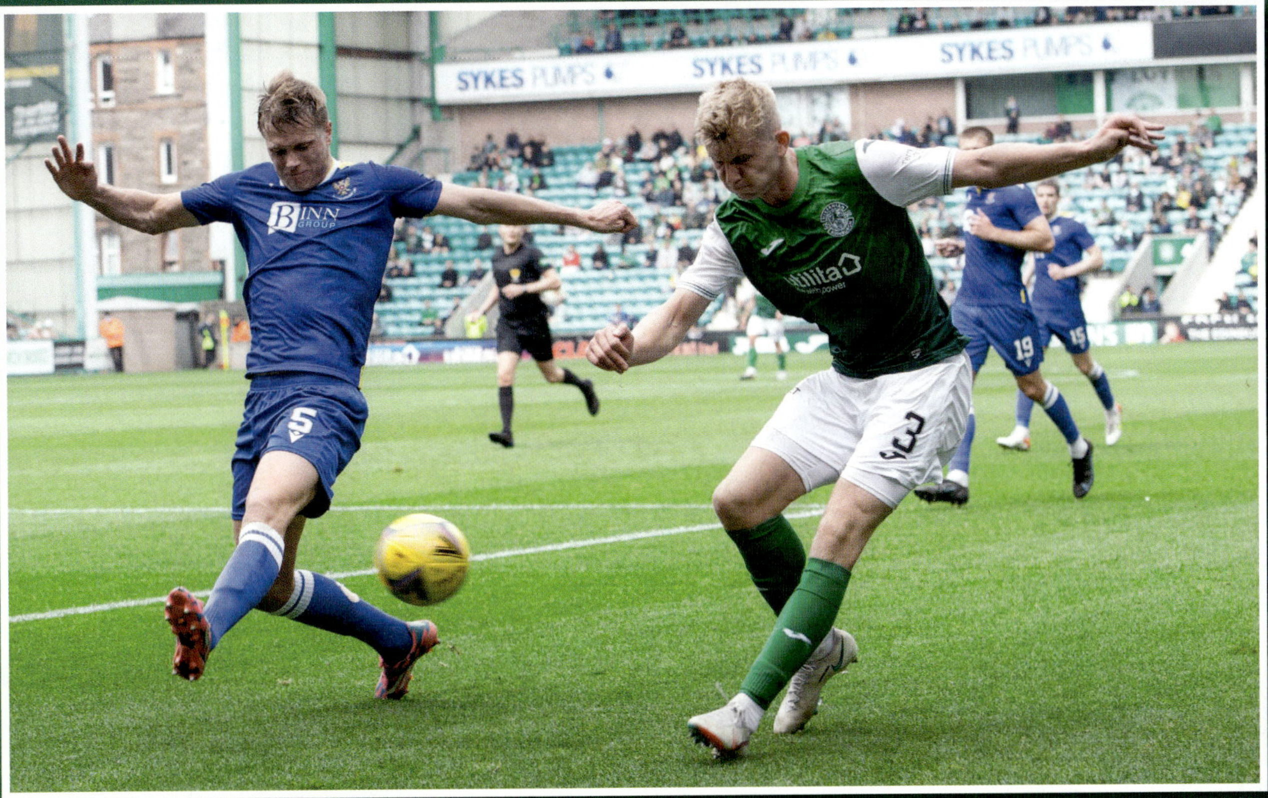

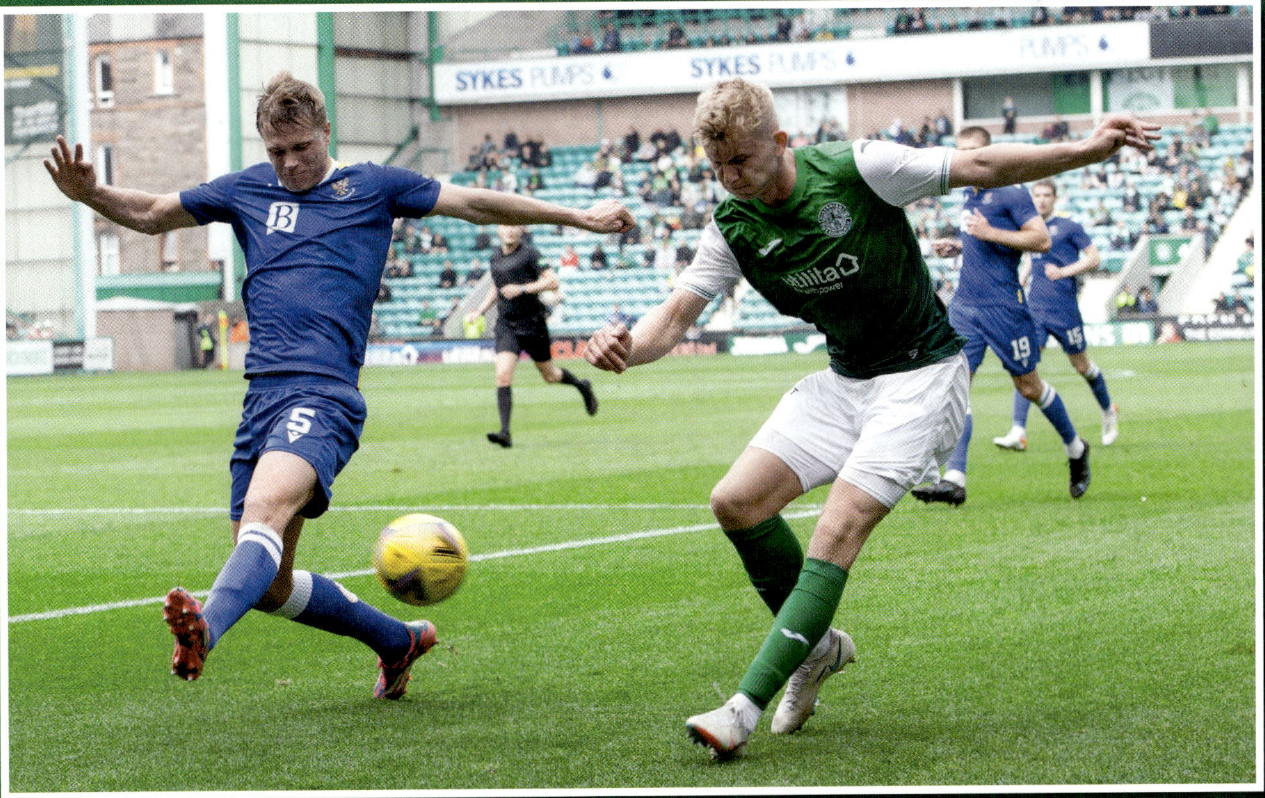

Answers on page 59.

DNIPRO KIDS

There was no bigger ovation on the night of Hibernian's Player of the Year awards than the one reserved for Stevie Carr. The face and driving force behind Dnipro Kids, Stevie was presented with the Unsung Hero award for their humanitarian work in Ukraine.

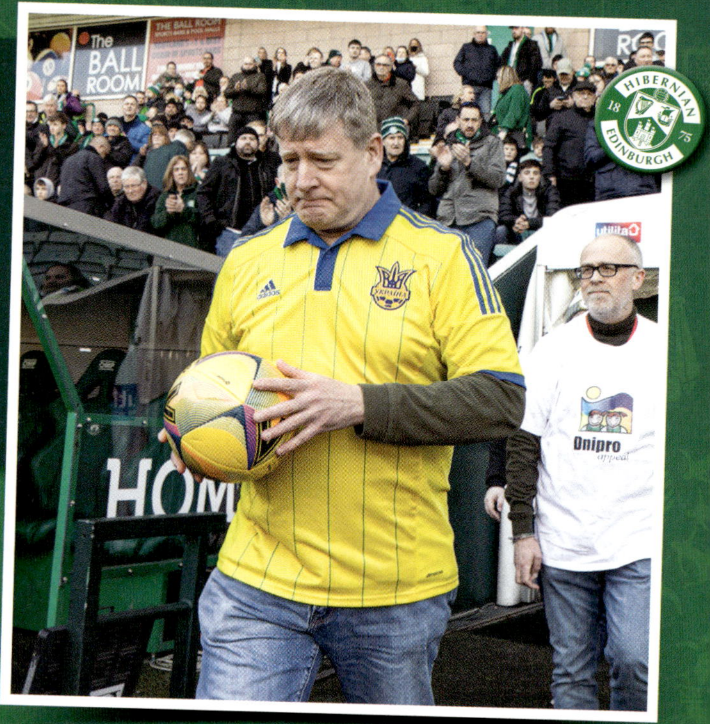

The recognition was thoroughly deserved for a group who have done so much to help some of those most in need of it, going right back to 2005.

When Hibs were drawn to play Dnipro Dnipropetrovsk in a UEFA Cup qualifier, few could have predicted the kind of lasting legacy the tie would produce.

Back then, a handful of supporters organised a charitable collection for local orphans.

So moved were they by their situation and story, a one-off donation quickly snowballed into a formal charity movement that's been running ever since.

Their generosity has enabled the purchase of clothing, medical equipment and even repairs to the building where they lived.

Their situation worsened given recent events, with Dnipro one of the cities left under siege.

Dnipro Kids – and the Hibernian family, behind them – rallied to the cause.

The Hanlon Stevenson Foundation – in conjunction with supporter groups and other Hibs-related online platforms – donated more than £52,000 to the cause.

Boosted by a single donation of £22,000 from Hibs.net.

Hibernian Women adapted their strip – wearing blue and yellow in support of Ukraine – with a fundraiser of their own dedicated to Dnipro Kids.

Figures within the club made their own private donations, in addition to a bucket collection in and around Easter Road Stadium.

Earlier this year, Stevie and the dedicated team behind Dnipro Kids played a key role in evacuating 50-plus children out of Ukraine to safety – securing safe passage and new lives in Scotland.

Those children were special guests of the club on the last day of the season, against St Johnstone – receiving a round of applause of their own from supporters who were in awe of their bravery and perseverance.

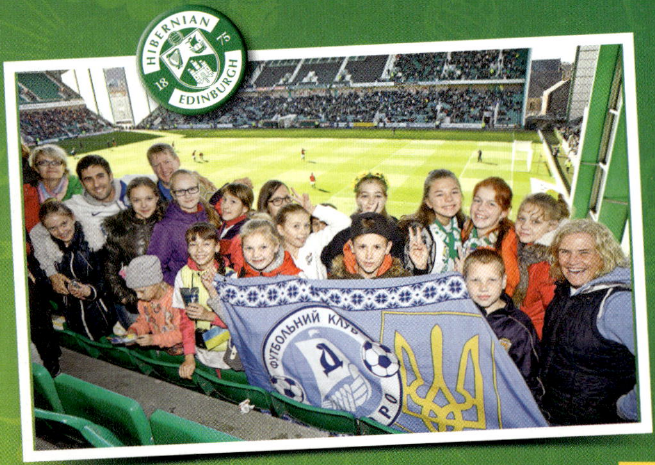

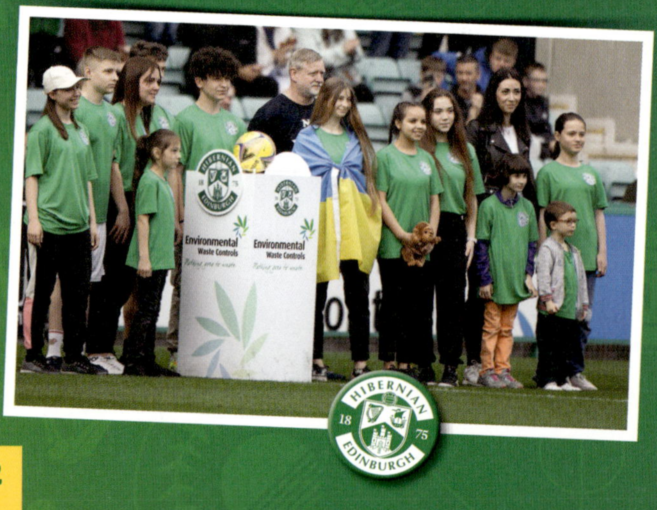

Stevie explained: *"We like to think that we make a big difference to their lives.*

"There's a lot of love between the kids in Ukraine and everyone involved with Dnipro Kids. Dnipro Kids is 100% all about the kids and the Hibernian supporters.

"We wouldn't have managed to keep going for as long as we have, and be able to do as much as we have, if it wasn't for the Hibs supporters.

"The supporters have taken Dnipro Kids into their hearts and view it as their charity. The kids in Dnipro have taken the Hibs supporters into their hearts as they have given them some unforgettable memories.

"The response from the Hibs supporters and the financial support we have received has been incredible. At the end of the day, we are just a small charity.

"But now, we are able to support the kids through this difficult time and provide a level of support to make sure they feel safe.

"One thing I would say is that this has completely been a team effort. I wouldn't have been able to do this all by myself. It would have been impossible for one person to do all this.

"We have only been able to help because we have a fantastic committee. We have supporters who regularly contribute funds and support the charity logistically. There have been so many people who have done so much for this project.

"So often people will put their hands up to volunteer and step up. That's how we get things done. It's kind of like a football team. It's a total team effort from everybody involved."

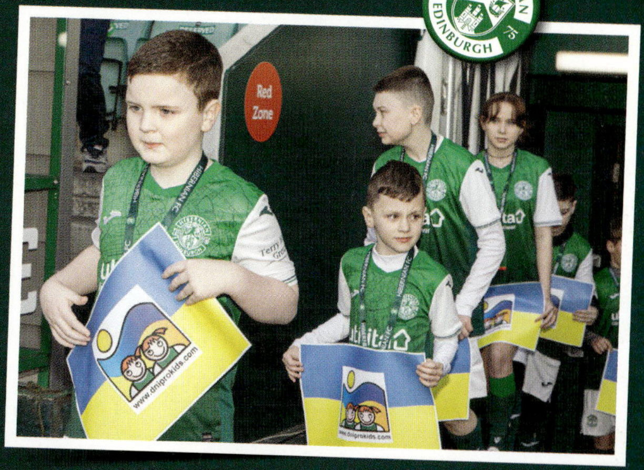

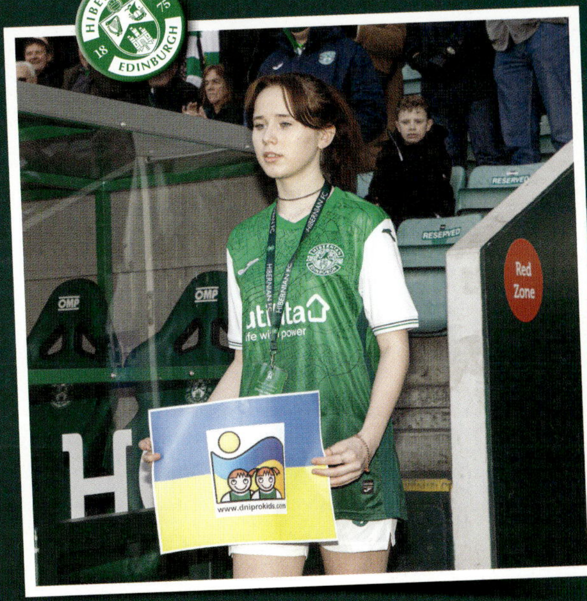

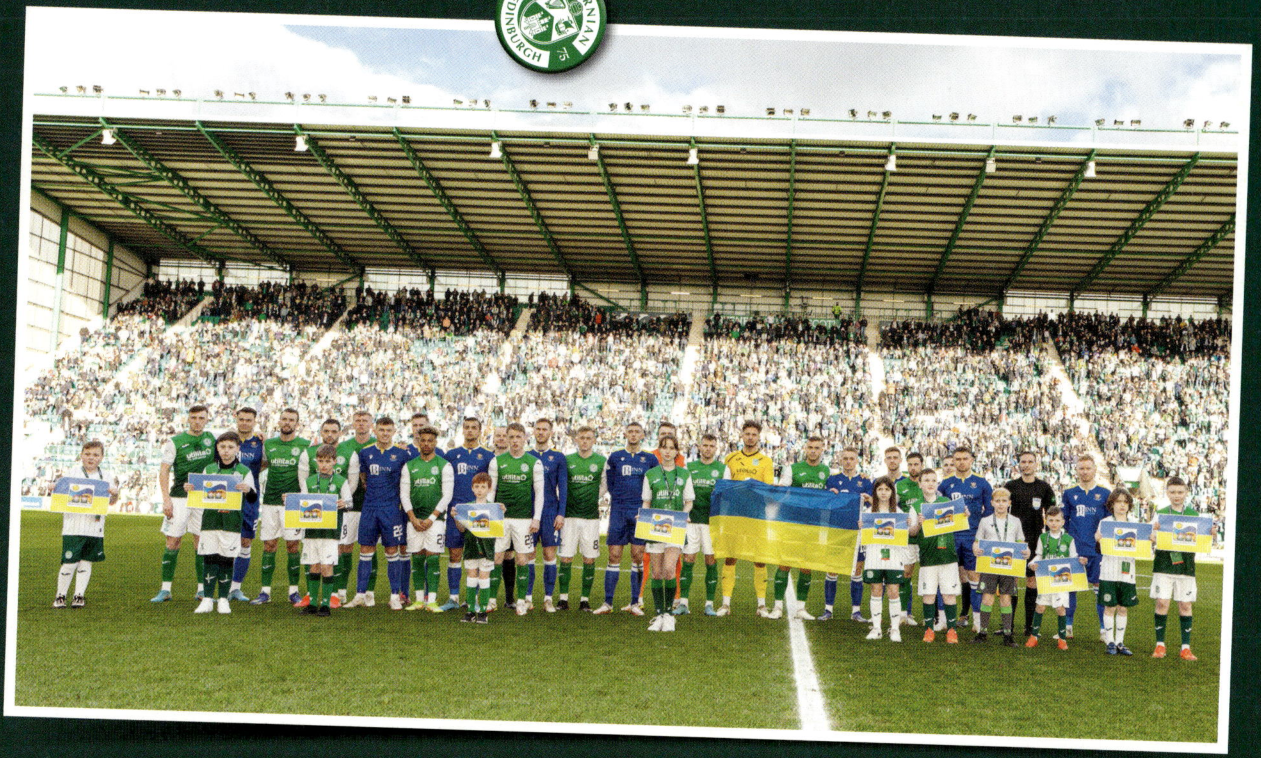

WORDSEARCH

Find the 12 Hibernian Academy graduates from within this wordsearch.

N	R	R	P	Y	P	J	C	C	N	Y	N	R	N	Q	L	D
W	E	T	E	R	T	L	O	R	T	D	M	V	V	N	T	K
O	K	M	B	H	B	N	W	S	V	M	B	W	A	F	E	R
R	A	G	C	R	C	D	O	Y	H	N	B	D	Q	V	M	X
B	T	K	H	L	T	T	T	L	T	O	R	T	I	N	K	F
T	T	E	M	C	G	H	E	G	N	O	C	N	W	X	F	S
T	I	N	J	V	N	T	W	L	I	A	T	O	P	V	M	U
O	H	N	P	N	U	N	K	R	F	H	H	Y	N	D	G	O
C	W	Y	D	D	O	C	K	N	O	N	G	L	J	N	K	E
S	N	M	M	T	Y	E	M	M	B	Y	E	K	U	Y	O	T
Q	E	I	F	N	R	T	S	N	N	F	K	V	H	A	X	R
V	V	L	G	E	O	O	J	Q	R	Y	Z	X	E	N	P	O
Y	E	L	D	M	N	M	B	L	Z	K	C	D	N	T	T	P
L	T	E	Z	T	N	F	P	M	B	G	G	R	B	X	S	N
V	S	R	N	Z	O	N	J	O	S	H	D	O	I	G	C	A
D	H	R	K	T	C	T	X	F	R	Q	N	V	W	T	R	Y
N	O	S	N	E	V	E	T	S	S	I	W	E	L	Y	V	R

Connor Young
Kenny Miller
Ryan Porteous
Derek Riordan
Kevin Thomson
Scott Brown
Josh Doig
Lewis Stevenson
Steven Fletcher
Josh O'Connor
Paul Hanlon
Steven Whittaker

Answers on page 59.

SUPPORTER LIAISON OFFICER

KIERAN POWER

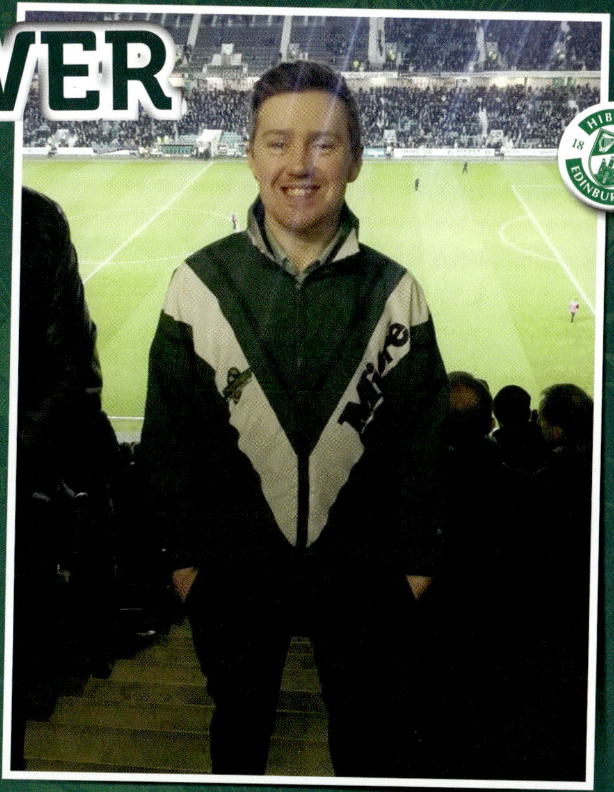

Kieran Power will be a familiar face to thousands of Hibernian supporters – as a home and away regular. He's helped thousands more in his role as Supporter Liaison Officer and, here, he explains a role that's a full-on labour of love.

How would you describe your role at Hibernian? What does it entail?

I'm the Supporters Liaison Officer for Hibernian in my spare time, around two other jobs. It's a varied role – providing customer service to supporters as a key club point of contact, query management and problem solving, mediator for conflict resolution and amplifying club communications. I'm a Jack of all trades, master of none in there.

On average, how many queries do you think you get through in an average month?

I track every query that comes to me, which allows me to spot trends, suggest improvements to the club departments or inform club management on a monthly basis. On average, it's anything between 200-300 queries a month covering a range of topics. It could be about anything – ticketing, match specifics, match safety, Clubstore enquiries, events, player requests or general feedback.

What's been the strangest request you've had to deal with?

Any request that comes to me has probably been sent for a genuine reason, whether it's surreal or not! I appreciate the time any supporter takes to get in touch. Being asked to open the stadium for Sonic The Hedgehog for a charity promotion photoshoot was out of the ordinary, but I was more than happy to oblige.

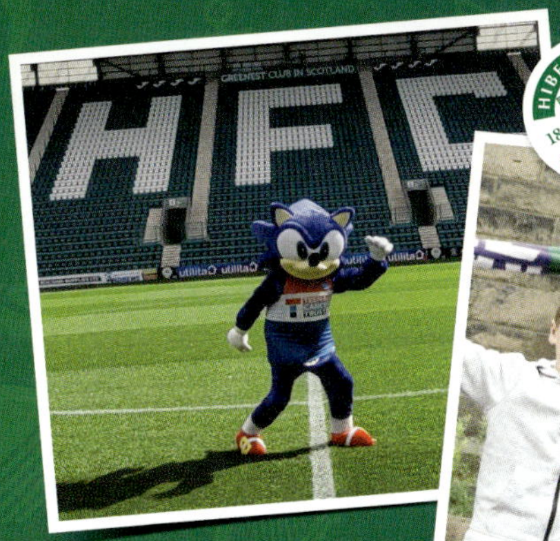

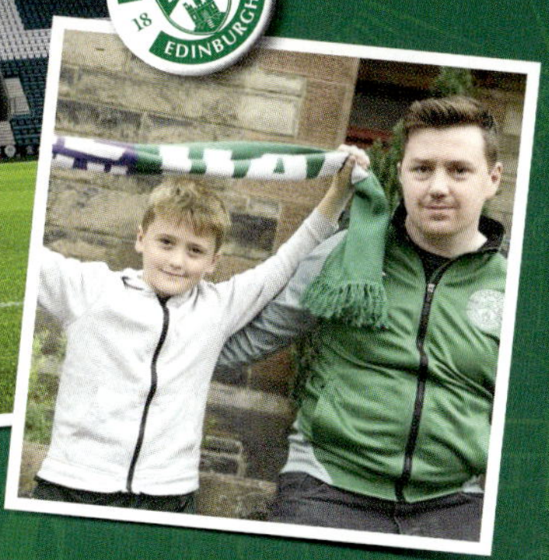

What's been the most heart-warming or rewarding one that's come in?

I thrive on problem-solving and helping fellow Hibs supporters out in any way – big or small. It brings me great satisfaction. I've been fortunate enough to help lots of Hibs fans with so many types of enquiries, from ticket collections to IT solutions, from first-ever games to those attending their final one at Easter Road. One that sticks out was opening up the stadium to a supporter who was going to lay flowers outside the West Stand in tribute to her late grandfather. I was last out of the stadium because of a non-matchday event, spoke to the supporter and took them to their grandfather's seat. When we were finished we left the flowers on that seat. Hibernian is for everyone and if I can play a small part in helping ensure someone's experience is a positive one, then I'm ecstatic.

You still sit with the supporters at games. What's your favourite away day?

I enjoy any Hibs away day. Our fans make for a great travelling support, vocally and in terms of the numbers who travel. I've enjoyed taking my son, and now my daughter, to away games with me. I get a buzz watching both take in stadiums for the first time. I'm a bit old-school and love being on the terracing compared to the all-seated modern stadiums. I really enjoyed Arbroath away in the Scottish Cup last season – the trip, the stadium and the local hospitality, despite it being the wettest day I've ever experienced at the football. Whatever the weather, it's always worth it.

Hibernian firsts

Hibernian has a proud history as one of Scotland's leading clubs and can point to more than a few examples of being pioneers within the game here.

Hibernian was the first British club to compete in European competition, reaching the final four of the European Cup in 1956. During that campaign, the legendary Eddie Turnbull became the first British player to score in European competition – netting in the 4-0 away win against German champions Rot-Weiss Essen.

The first ever women's international football match between Scotland and England was hosted at Hibernian Park on May 7, 1881. It's now the Sunnyside premises of the Hibernian Supporters Association.

In 1977, Hibs became the first Scottish club to display a sponsor's logo on their shirt and, three years later, were the first in the country to install undersoil heating.

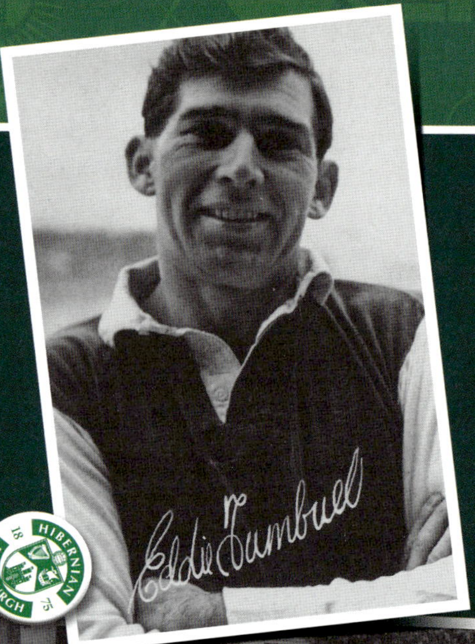

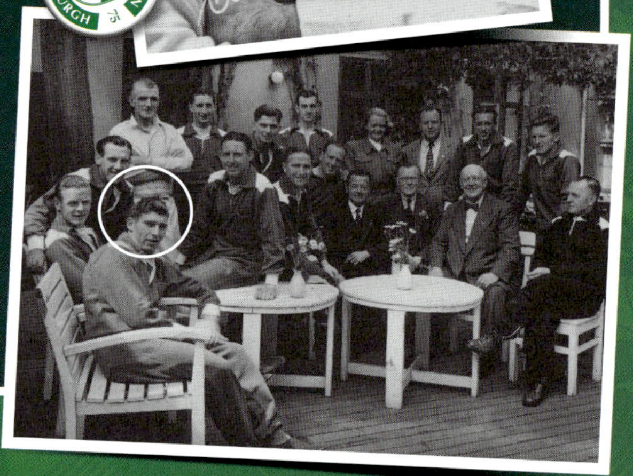

Leagues

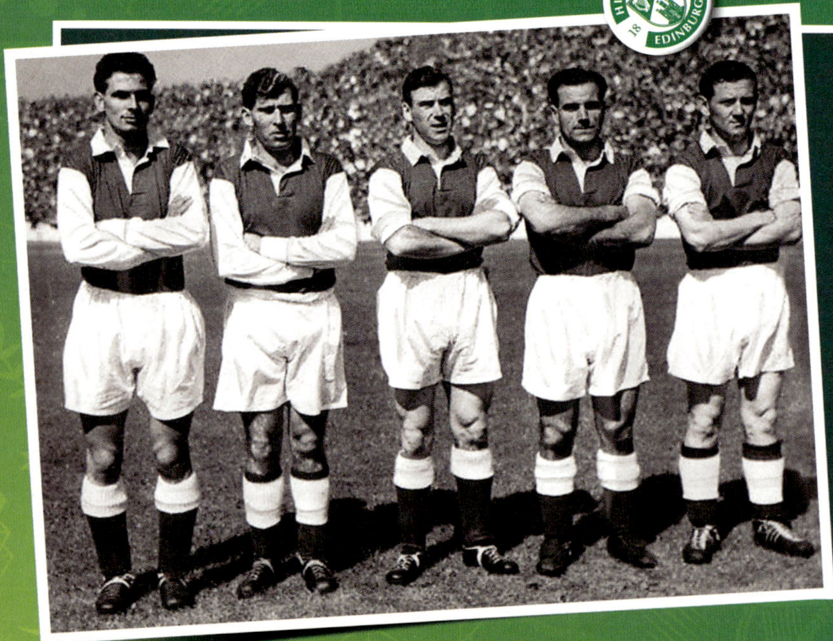

While Scotland's top-flight is now known as the Scottish Premiership, from 1890-1975 it was referred to as Scottish Division One. During that period, Hibernian won the league four times – in 1903, then later in 1948, 1951 and 1952, in no small part thanks to the heroics of The Famous Five. Hibernian have been runners-up six times, in 1897, 1947, 1950, 1953, 1974 and 1975.

The Scottish Cup

The club has won the Scottish Cup three times – in 1887, 1902 and, famously, in 2016. That day at Hampden Park saw current first-team coach David Gray head a dramatic late winner against Rangers. It ended an agonising wait for success in the tournament, but anyone who was there that day in Glasgow will probably tell you it was worth the wait!

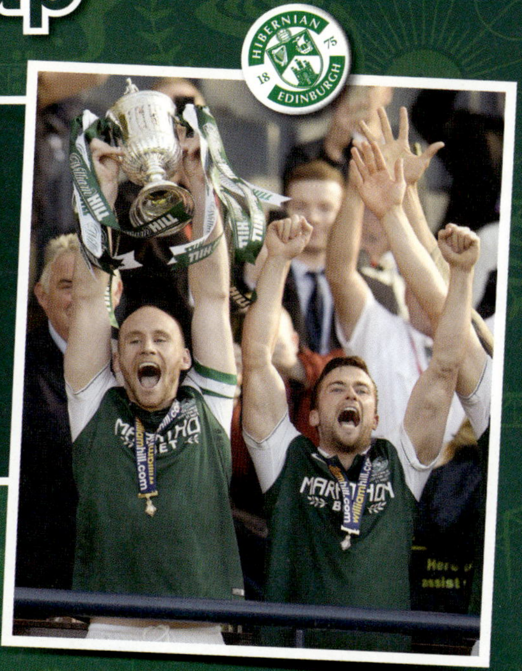

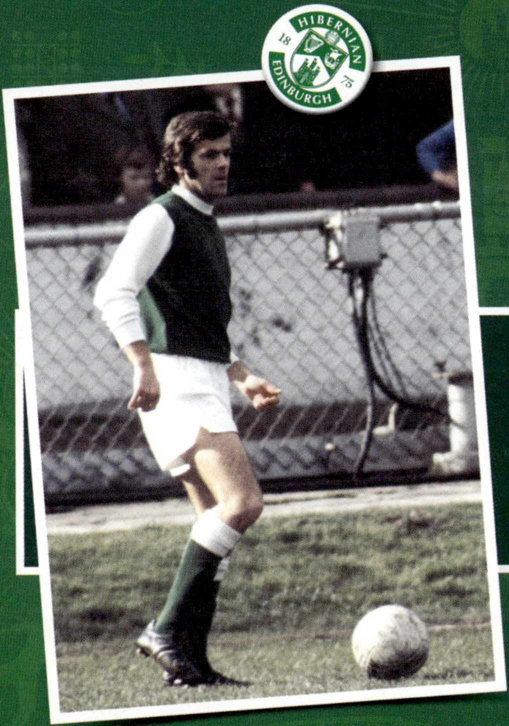

The League Cup

Three League Cup triumphs have been secured throughout the club's history – in 1972, 1991 and 2007. Pat Stanton, Murdo MacLeod and Rob Jones captaining Hibs on those occasions and have spoken repeatedly about just how much it meant to them.

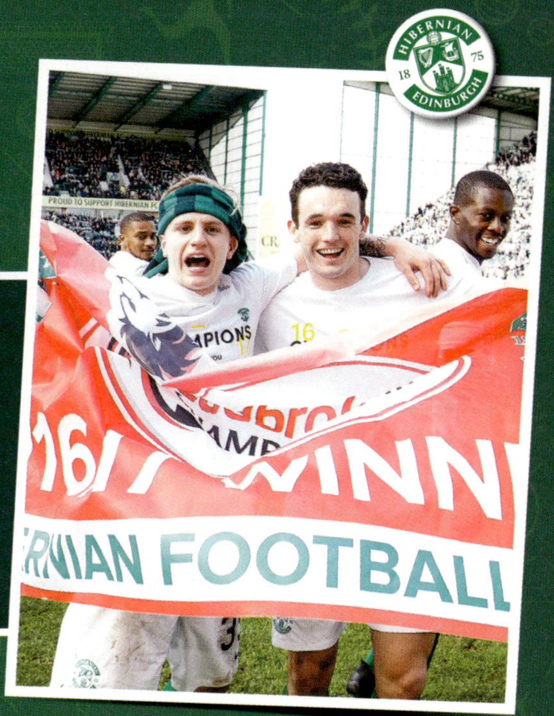

Minor Honours

The club also won the second tier of Scottish league football (now known as The Championship and previously as Division Two) on six occasions – in 1894, 1895, 1933, 1981, 1999 and 2017. The Drybrough Cup was won in 1972 and 1973, the Summer Cup in 1941 and 1964, and the Southern League Cup in 1944.

ANSWERS

p16-17 Season Quiz

1. FC Santa Coloma.
2. Kevin Dabrowski.
3. Fulham.
4. Arbroath.
5. Eddie May.
6. Lewis Stevenson.
7. Dundalk.
8. Aberdeen.
9. Elias Melkersen.
10. Martin Boyle.
11. Paul McGinn.
12. Josh Campbell and Josh Doig.
13. Jake Doyle-Hayes.
14. Kilmarnock.

p34 Who Am I?

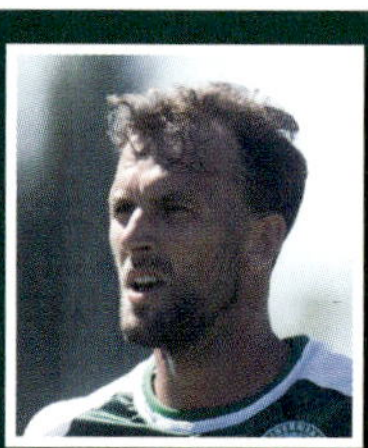

1 - Christian Doidge

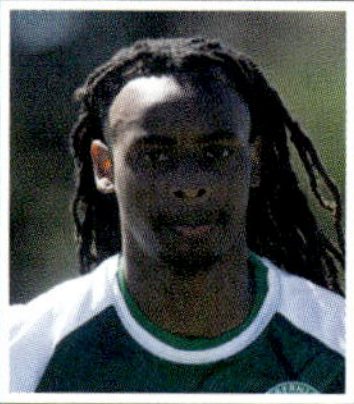

2 - Jair Taveres

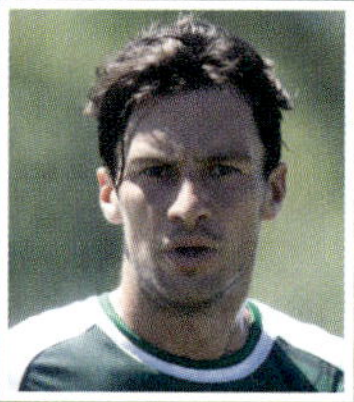

3 - Joe Newell

p42 Spot The Ball

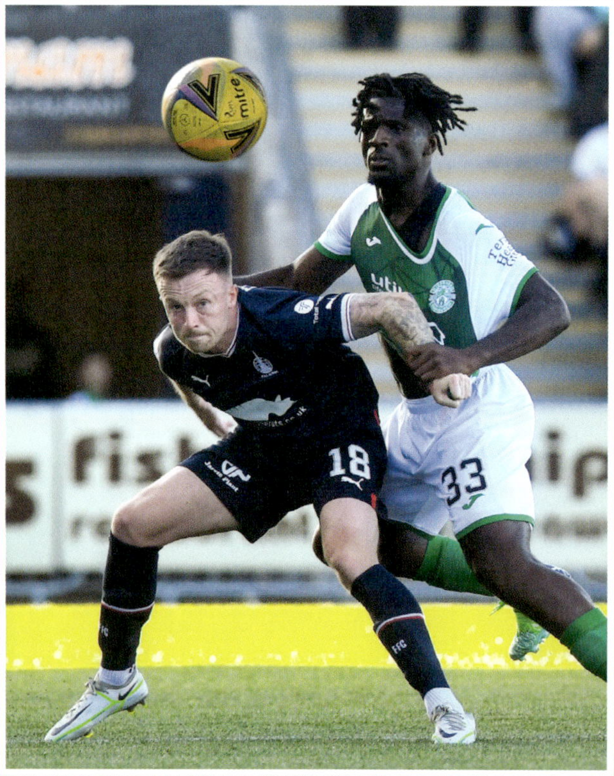

p46-47 Player Chat

1 – Lewis Stevenson – E

2 – Lee Johnson – H

3 – Kevin Dabrowski – F

4 – Elias Melkersen – D

5 – Demetri Mitchell – B

6 – Aiden McGeady – G

7 – David Marshall – J

8 – Allan Delferriere – C

9 – Darren McGregor – A

10 – Chris Cadden – I

p51 Spot The Difference

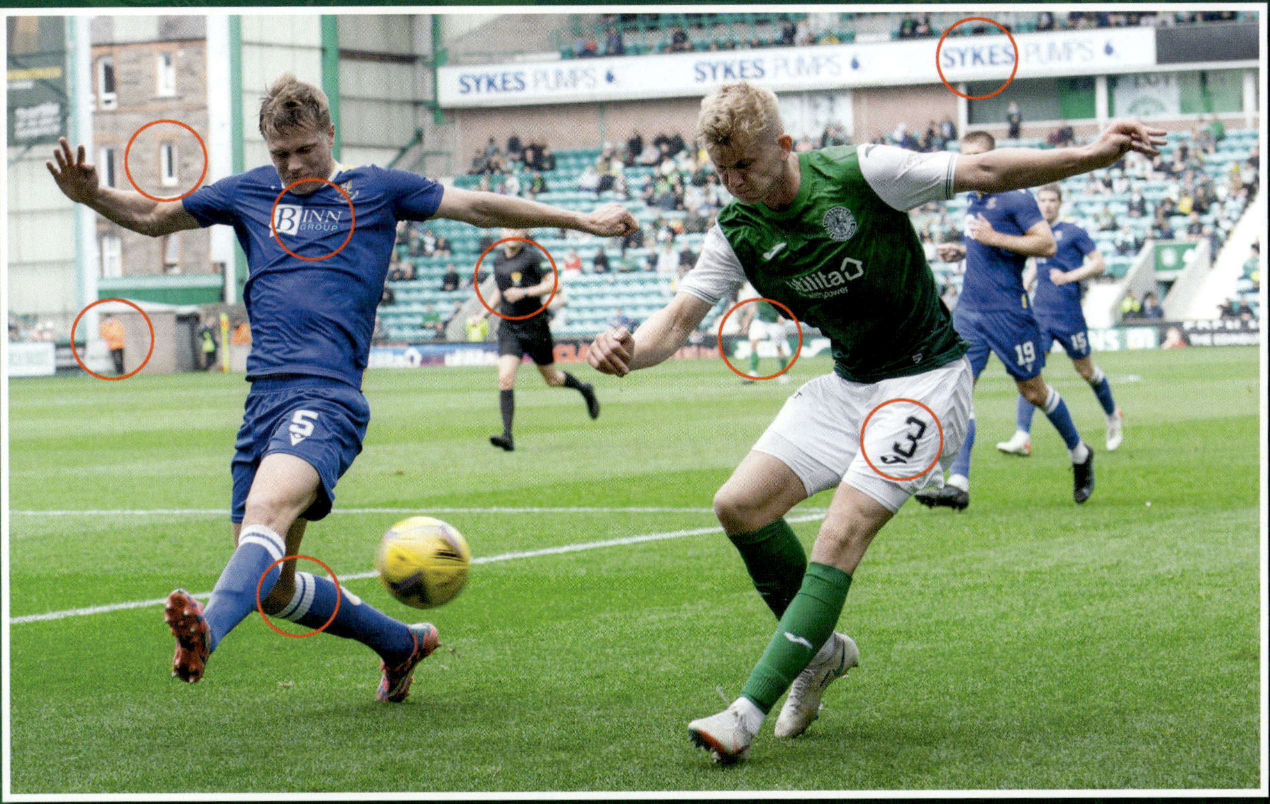

p54 Wordsearch

N	R	R	P	Y	P	J	C	C	N	Y	N	R	N	Q	L	D
W	E	T	E	R	T	L	O	R	T	D	M	V	V	N	T	K
O	K	M	B	H	B	N	W	S	V	M	B	W	A	F	E	R
R	A	G	C	R	C	D	O	Y	H	N	B	D	Q	V	M	X
B	T	K	H	L	T	T	T	L	T	O	R	T	I	N	K	F
T	T	E	M	C	G	H	E	G	N	O	C	N	W	X	F	S
T	I	N	J	V	N	T	W	L	I	A	T	O	P	V	M	U
O	H	N	P	N	U	N	K	R	F	H	H	Y	N	D	G	O
C	W	Y	D	D	O	C	K	N	O	N	G	L	J	N	K	E
S	N	M	M	T	Y	E	M	M	B	Y	E	K	U	Y	O	T
Q	E	I	F	N	R	T	S	N	N	F	K	V	H	A	X	R
V	V	L	G	E	O	O	J	Q	R	Y	Z	X	E	N	P	O
Y	E	L	D	M	N	M	B	L	Z	K	C	D	N	T	T	P
L	T	E	Z	T	N	F	P	M	B	G	G	R	B	X	S	N
V	S	R	N	Z	O	N	J	O	S	H	D	O	I	G	C	A
D	H	R	K	T	C	T	X	F	R	Q	N	V	W	T	R	Y
N	O	S	N	E	V	E	T	S	S	I	W	E	L	Y	V	R

Connor Young
Derek Riordan
Josh Doig
Josh O'Connor
Kenny Miller
Kevin Thomson
Lewis Stevenson
Paul Hanlon
Ryan Porteous
Scott Brown
Steven Fletcher
Steven Whittaker

CONTACT INFORMATION

Stadium Address:
Easter Road Stadium,
12 Albion Place,
Edinburgh, EH7 5QG

club@hibernianfc.co.uk

0131 661 2159

Social Media

Hibernian Football Club Official

HibernianFootballClub

Hibernianwomen

@HibernianFC

Hibernian FC

Hibernian FC

www.hibernianfc.co.uk

Ticket Office
Email: tickets@hibernianfc.co.uk

Opening Hours:
Monday to Friday, 10am-5pm
(via email and telephone)
Monday - Friday 10am - 4pm in person

Clubstore
Email: info@hiberniandirect.co.uk
Telephone: 0131 656 7078

Hospitality
Email: hospitality@hibernianfc.co.uk

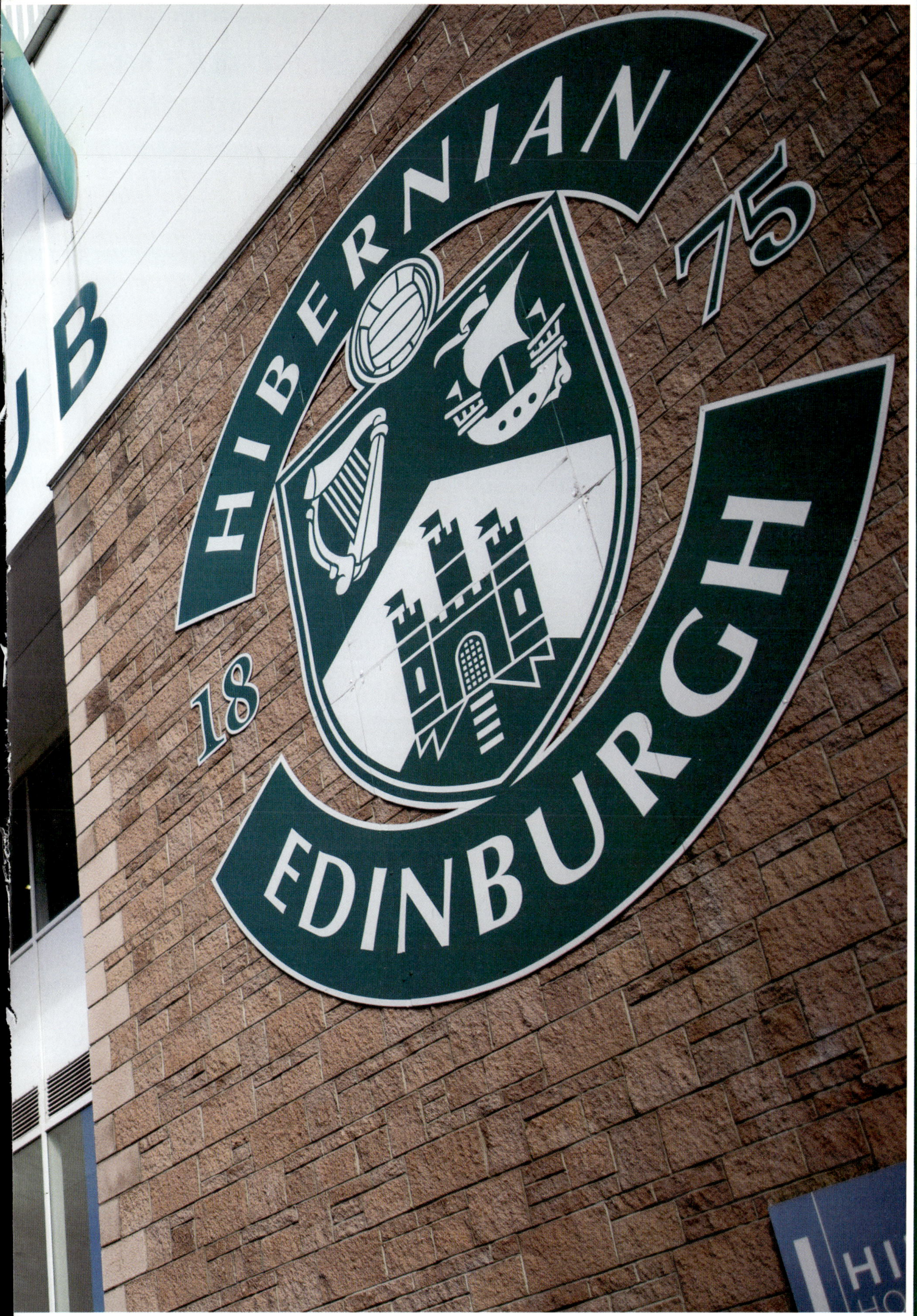
HIBERNIAN
18
75
EDINBURGH

CELEBRATION TIME

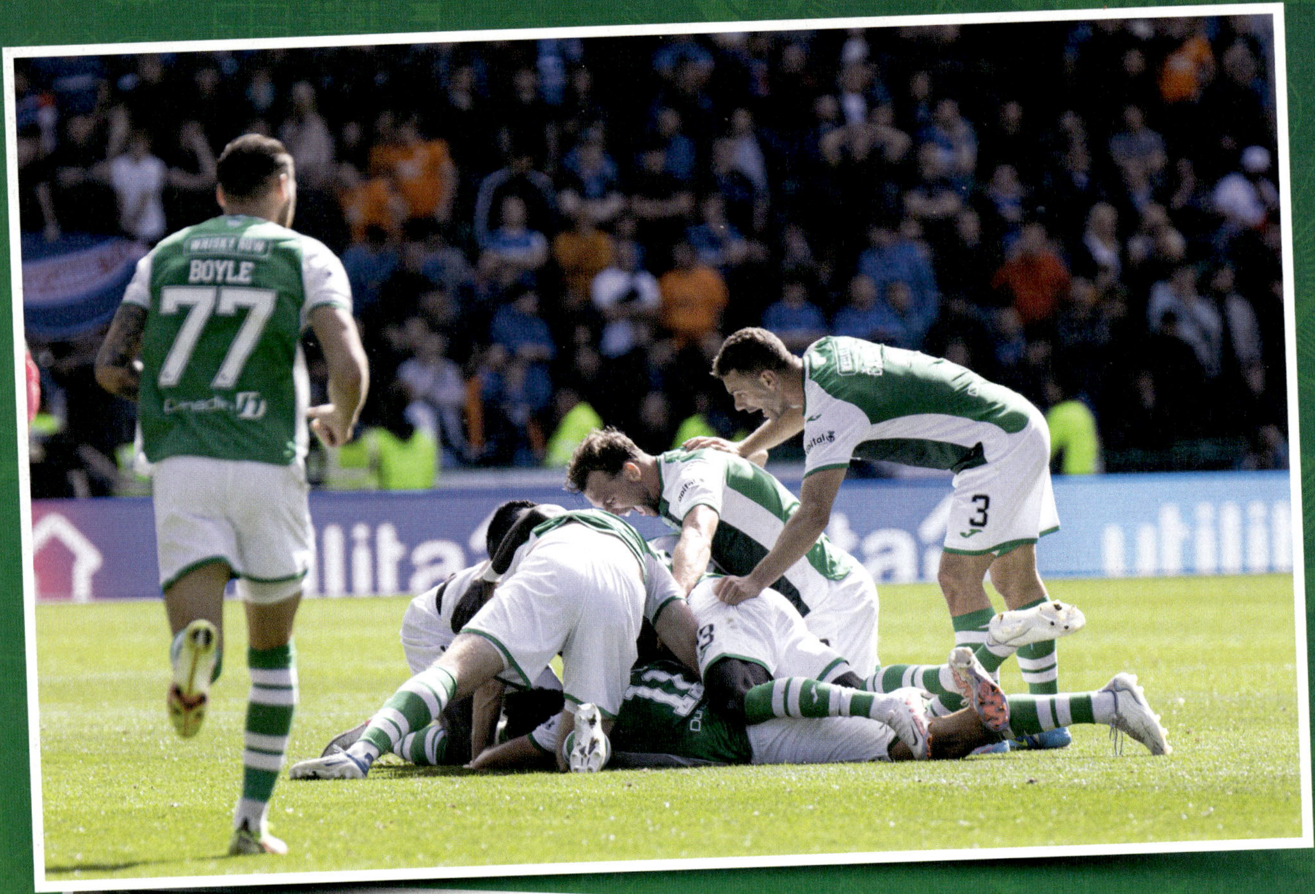

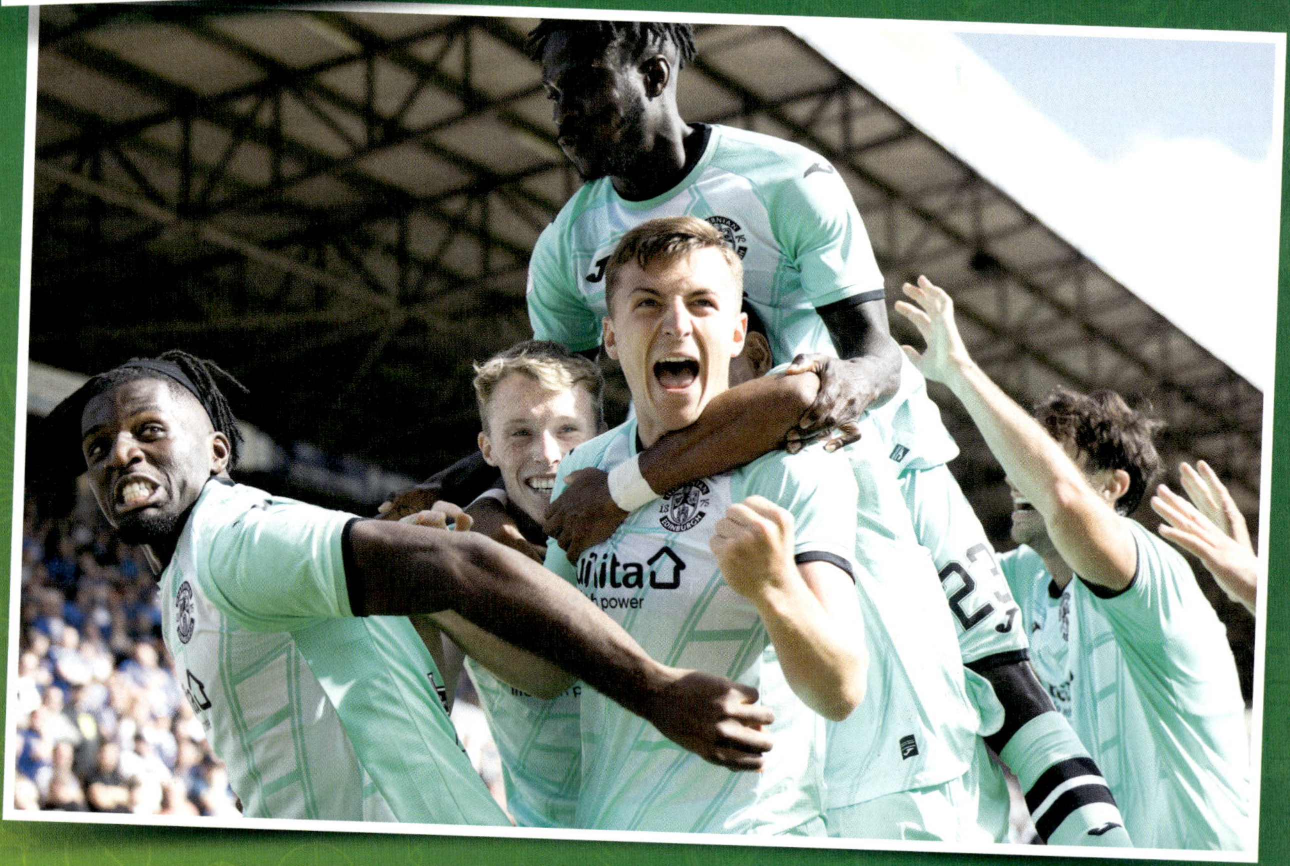